P9-CNE-037

WITH AXE AND FLASK

WITH AXE AND FLASK

The History of Persephone Township
from Pre-Cambrian Times to the Present

Dan Needles

(with excerpts from the pioneering work of D.J. Goulding, M.D.)

Macfarlane Walter & Ross
Toronto

Copyright © 2002 by Dan Needles

All rights reserved. No part of this book may be reproduced, transmitted in any form or by any means, electronic, mechanical, photocopying, recording, or otherwise without written permission from the publisher (or in the case of photocopying or other reprographic copying, a licence from a licensing body such as the Canadian Copyright Licensing Agency), except by a reviewer, who may quote brief passages in a review.

Macfarlane Walter & Ross
An Affiliate of McClelland & Stewart Ltd.
37A Hazelton Avenue
Toronto, Canada M5R 2E3
www.mwandr.com

National Library of Canada Cataloguing in Publication

Needles, Dan
With axe and flask : the history of Persephone Township
from pre-cambrian times to the present / Dan Needles.

ISBN 1-55199-088-1

I. Title.

PS8577.E333W58 2002   C813'.54   C2002-902836-1
PR9199.3.N327W58 2002

Macfarlane Walter & Ross gratefully acknowledges support for its publishing program from the Canada Council for the Arts, the Ontario Arts Council, and the Government of Canada through the Book Publishing Industry Development Program.

Printed and bound in Canada

To D.J. and Bill

The stories and legends of *With Axe and Flask* did not all tumble out of my fertile brain. Inspiration came from many sources, including Marie Cruickshank, of the Collingwood Public Library, who unearthed all sorts of juicy tidbits from archives, as did Steve Brown and Wayne Townsend, of the Dufferin County Museum. The rest of the material has been gathered patiently at arborite kitchen tables in Mono, Mulmur, and Nottawasaga Townships over the past fifty years.

Special thanks to my editor, Rick Archbold, for steering *With Axe and Flask* from a one-line reference in the Wingfield Plays into a book and, in the process, reminding me why we are such good friends. And to Rick Feldman, who fed and housed me through two months of rewrites.

My copy editor, Barbara Czarnecki, insisted that Persephone be as real a place as possible. Douglas Beattie, Rod Beattie, and Roger Hall read the text and made many helpful suggestions. Any errors that remain are mine.

Finally, a sincere thank you to my wife, Heath, who ran the house and farm while I completed this book and then took me back in when it was all done.

D.N.

CONTENTS

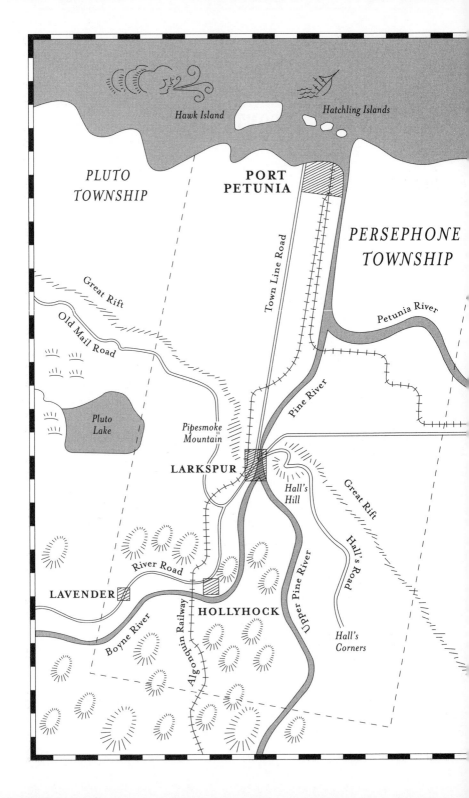

GEORGIAN BAY

DEMETER TOWNSHIP

N

KEMPENFELDT

Ontario, Simcoe,
and Huron Railway

DEMETER
CENTRE

New Military Road

Petunia
River Bridge

PERSEPHONE TOWNSHIP IN 1860

Drumlins		Swamp or Marsh	
——— Road		Forest	
River			
++++ Railway		Town	

1 mile

PREFACE

The wind in Persephone Township has a way of sweeping you off your feet when you least expect it. It will come out of nowhere and flatten you against a shop window on the main street of Larkspur or tear the car door handle out of your grasp when you stop at the mailbox at the end of your lane. The township itself is a bit like that wind. It carries you away when you least expect it. Take the writing of this book, for instance. It all happened quite by accident that I was abducted by Persephone.

Last spring I took the train from the city to Larkspur to clear up some family business involving my grandfather's estate. He and my grandmother lived in a Victorian brick cottage on five manicured acres where the Boyne River meets the Pine River in Larkspur. In his will, he left this property to the town as a park, but now the town was whining about the expense of maintaining it and was trying to wiggle out from under the strict obligations of the trust deed. As the only surviving member of the family in the country, I'd agreed to represent the Goulding interests while the fate of the park was decided.

I had hoped to wrap things up in a couple of days, but the mills of municipal government in this community seem to run on geological time, so I ended up drawing on my vacation allowance and extending my stay at the Commercial Hotel on Wellington Street to a week. I spent the evenings reading magazines in my room or playing darts in the Ladies and Escorts Lounge.

I was in no particular rush to get back to the city. I had been involved in an ugly interoffice skirmish at the government public relations office where I was working at the time, and I was facing a rather difficult career choice – as in whether to have one. But counting cars on Wellington Street from my hotel room was not on my top ten list of favourite vacation experiences.

By Sunday morning, after several more days of inconclusive meetings and more evening dart games than I would care to count, I decided I needed some exercise. So I took a stroll down Wellington Street. As I approached St. Luke's Anglican Church, where my grandparents used to drag me every summer Sunday of my adolescent years, I could hear through the open windows the congregation singing "Softly and Tenderly Jesus Is Calling." This is not one of my favourite hymns, but I peeked in the door for old time's sake. All heads turned and the minister beamed such a beatific smile of welcome that I felt obliged to take a seat in the empty back pew.

I endured the readings and two more hymns, but when the minister dug out a wad of sermon notes and knelt before the altar to pray for stamina, instinct prompted me to duck downstairs to the church basement where the children used to take Sunday school.

The room was much as I remembered it, still housing a kitchen, long trestle tables for pancake suppers, and an ancient oil furnace. The fragrances of jellied salad, tuna casserole, and heating oil infused the cool dank air. I noticed that the Noah's Ark poster I had worked on for the church centennial in 1963 was still hanging on the wall. Beside it was a row of faded watercolours illuminating the high points of the Israelites' flight out of Egypt. I followed the Exodus story down to the far corner by the furnace, where my foot stubbed against an obstacle. I stooped to see a thick clothbound volume supporting one end of the furnace oil tank. On the spine of the book, in faded gold letters, I could just make out the name D.J. Goulding, M.D.

This was a startling coincidence. Dr. Goulding was my grandfather. What on earth would he have written a book about? Using a stack of old hymnals as a fulcrum and a loose board from one of the trestle tables as a lever, I was able to pry up the tank far enough to remove the ancient volume and replace it with two copies of *The Book of Alternative Services*. Then I took my discovery to the light to examine it.

The ravages of time, oil spills, and basement floodings had taken their toll – many pages were stuck together and whole sections were illegible. But the title page was still decipherable. It read: *With Axe and Flask: The History of Persephone Township from Pre-Cambrian Times to the Present*. It was self-published and had been printed by the Larkspur *Free Press & Economist* in 1933. Now this really was quite extraordinary. I'd had no inkling my grandfather had been a writer. If I'd expected anything, it would have been some obscure medical text, not a local history.

The next day, when I made enquiries at the Larkspur Town Library, I was little the wiser. The library carries in its local history section a number of pamphlets and photograph collections, but the librarian had never seen a copy of my grandfather's book. Come to think of it, though, she had heard several older residents mention a volume of local history that had been written in the late 1920s or early

1930s. That was it. She then guided me to the newspaper files, where I looked up my grandfather's obituary. (He died while I was away at university, so I'd missed his funeral.) I discovered the following:

Larkspur
Dec. 11, 1973
Dr. D.J. Goulding, late of this parish, entered into rest on Thursday last after a short illness and was interred in the Anglican cemetery after a memorial service held in St. Luke's Church. Goulding was a tireless man of science who tended to his patients faithfully without regard to their social standing or worldly wealth. He died lamented by the community and an example to all who would aspire to the care and comfort of the sick.

The only shadow that fell across his otherwise unblemished life was his unfortunate foray some years ago into the realm of literature, which resulted in the publication of a controversial volume of history documenting the early days of the community. The good doctor erred in assuming that the passage of time had clouded people's memories about certain incidents and personalities and that it was safe to place these matters under a public lens. In the resulting acrimony his practice was somewhat diminished.

Nonetheless, a large crowd attended his obsequies and several leading citizens paid tribute to his unflinching dedication to the principles of Hippocrates. At the interment, a box of his beloved history books was placed in the grave at the foot of the coffin and committed with him to the earth. The crowd then retired to the Commercial Hotel to give thanks for a full life fully lived. Posterity's verdict will no doubt record that he was a man ahead of his time.

My first reaction to reading these words was guilt that I hadn't been at the funeral. My second was annoyance that my grandfather had been treated so roughly by the towns- people because of an honest attempt to capture their com- munal heritage. I'd known Dr. Goulding as a genial man. He must have been a patient one as well, to have tolerated a bored teenager summer after summer.

After another frustrating day dealing with Hillview offi- cialdom, I skipped my after-dinner darts game and went straight to my room to read my grandfather's book. I was still reading as dawn broke and birds began chirping in the ancient maples on Wellington Street outside my window. The book was more interesting than I'd expected.

When I checked for e-mail on my laptop that morning, I discovered that my employer had taken the courageous decision to forge ahead into the twenty-first century with- out my services. It seemed that my career path had once again led me to the off-ramp of the information highway. I sent a note to a friend in my apartment building, asking him to water the plants till I got back. That evening I returned to my reading.

On Friday night, exactly one week after arriving in Larkspur, I was sitting at the bar of the Commercial Hotel, where I was hard at work sweating the pages of Dr. Goulding's book apart and making notes on a pad of yellow paper. Pete and Jamie, a couple of weather-beaten cattle farmers who had gained some respect for my skill at the dartboard, climbed onto stools on either side of me and asked what I was doing.

"Just reading," I replied.

"It must be nice to have nothing to do and all day to do it," said Jamie.

"Actually, I'm doing some research."

"Ooooh, yeah," said Pete, in that singsong way that the residents have when there is no obvious reply to what has just been said. "Cure for cancer?"

There was a pause. Then, in one of those strange paroxysms that have marked my career path to date, I blurted out, "I'm writing a book. It's called *With Axe and Flask*. It's a history of Persephone Township."

The music stopped, the bartender looked over the top of his copy of the *Auction Register*, and heads turned from the card tables.

"Don't worry," I said. "It's all ancient history."

Later, when I thought it over, writing a book seemed as good an occupation as any while I was "between successes," as we say in the public relations field. But if I was going to write a local history, I figured I'd better have an angle of attack – what my university professors called a thesis. I have always been an avid reader of history, and my undergraduate major at the University of Toronto was political economy. This background, together with a brief stint in the newspaper business and, most recently, a slightly longer stint as a speechwriter for a now-forgotten minister of culture in a short-lived provincial government, makes me more qualified than many who write local histories these days.

Thanks to this varied resumé, I know a thing or two my grandfather didn't. In History 101, for example, I learned that about the time Dr. Goulding was writing his book, the traditional approach to history as a procession of dates and events was being challenged by the work of the great Canadian historian Harold Innis. Innis introduced the world to the staple thesis, which demonstrated that the fur trade, the fisheries, and the timber industry gave us a political tradition that was distinctively Canadian and quite different from that of the United States. The staple thesis was in many ways a response to the frontier thesis of the American historian Frederick Jackson Turner, which tells us we're all looking for greener pastures. In the 1960s the survival thesis of Margaret Atwood came into vogue. In it Atwood posits that an illogical fear of freezing to death in the dark animates most Canadian writers and artists. None of these paradigms had much effect on the one-damn-thing-after-another approach taken by the school system that I grew up in and from which so many of my contemporaries fled in favour of shop and hockey.

After considering each of these possibilities, I decided that not one of them seemed right for Persephone. So I turned to the often-overlooked hypothesis of the historian Michael Bliss, which I stumbled across during a second-year university course with the optimistic title "The Evolution of Canadian Business." Professor Bliss described Canada as a land of *limited* opportunity where smart people are satisfied with a steady 2 to 3 percent annual real return on their investment. He observed that our economic history has been enlivened by a long parade of fast-talking moneymen, pirates, second-storey artists, and speculators who force the pace of economic development, with the active encouragement of the government, in a way that alarms the more prudent entrepreneurs who have already been through a couple of winters here. They invariably come to a bad end, but not before they have emptied their neighbours' wallets and exhausted the reserve fund of the nearest public body. From Martin Frobisher struggling home across the North Atlantic in 1577 with a hold full of worthless iron pyrite for

Elizabeth I through to the salted ore samples of the Bre-X gold mining scandal of 1997, there is a remarkable similarity in the pattern of their schemes. Together, such ruffians help to explain why the eminent philosopher and literary critic Northrop Frye was inspired to christen Canada "a land of ruins." Frye observed that, as a people, we come to a place, use it up, and move on, which makes our history "a long procession of leave-takings."* Many of these departures occur in the middle of the night, down the back stairs with a satchel full of cash. In Persephone Township, the landscape is dotted with the remnants of many of these failed visions.

For my money, Michael Bliss with a dash of Northrop Frye offers the paradigm with the best fuel economy and a roomy interior, and it is in this vehicle that I've chosen to tour Persephone Township and its rich past.

I understand from the owner of the *Free Press & Economist*, who rented a room to me in the Bell Block on Wellington Street, that many out-of-township readers of the long-running weekly column "Letter from Wingfield Farm" have expressed interest in the precise location of Larkspur and of Persephone Township itself. A number have reported their failed attempts to reach Larkspur by car, even in good weather. The Pine River Bridge Reconstruction Project, begun in 1965 and scheduled to be completed soon, should make the trip easier and eliminate the lengthy detour through the drumlins.

But a new challenge to the traveller has presented itself, with the recent amalgamation of the municipalities of Larkspur, Port Petunia, and Persephone Township into

---

* At least, people tell me that Frye said this and I have no reason to doubt their word, not having read Frye myself.

a single municipality that now travels under the uninspired name of Township of Hillview. So many roads have been renamed and renumbered that the locals themselves can't give coherent directions to one another. Readers who get close enough to ask directions, however, need to know that the locals pronounce the name of the township in two syllables, "Purse-foan," and refer to themselves as "Purse-foan-ites." Persephonites have not taken kindly to the removal of the old signposts, and each time the road department puts up a sign for Hillview, someone creeps out under cover of darkness and cuts it off at ground level with a chain saw. The amalgamated Hillview Township Council has pretty much given up trying to replace these signs, and you can now drive right through Persephone without knowing it.

However, if you just get in a car and drive north of Toronto for a couple of hours or so, many of the places mentioned in this book ought to become easily recognizable. You will know you are in Persephone when the wind hits you full in the face and there are cows on the road.

Raymond Denton
Larkspur
April 2002

ACKNOWLEDGMENTS

A part from the standard reference material and land records in public archives and the Land Registry Office, there are numerous sources of public and private information about the early years of settlement in Persephone. Unfortunately, many large gaps exist because of the Great Fire of 1885, which destroyed the Larkspur Town Hall and some of the early township archives. This is not to be confused with the Great Fire in the fall of 1976, when the township clerk burned fourteen boxes of material in his back yard just before the Ministry of Municipal Affairs arrived to investigate the township finances. I was able to draw on town and township council minutes dating back to the 1840s; back issues of various newspapers published in Larkspur and Port Petunia; proceedings of the Larkspur Orange Lodge; and a number of pamphlets and restaurant placemats that have been written about certain events and sites in the township's history. Recent discoveries, including the scrapbooks, expedition notes, and campaign literature of Charles Augustus Fortescue, the hope chest of Isabella Pargeter, and the diaries of Fanny Haddock, have proven enlightening and invaluable.

There is a strong oral tradition among Persephonites, one that I was able to tap into during breakfasts at the Red

Hen Restaurant and evenings with the regulars at the Commercial Hotel. I particularly appreciate the kindness of this latter establishment, which provided me with a regular space at the bar, where I was allowed to work undisturbed for weeks at a time. In addition, I conducted a number of personal interviews and rummaged through many trunks in many attics looking for local colour.

I have also been very fortunate in securing the assistance of Ms. Doreen Cameron, the part-time archivist at the Larkspur library, who also works afternoons as a secretary-receptionist in the offices of the *Free Press & Economist*. It was she who brought to ground many of the primary sources that have allowed me to build on my grandfather's foundation. She has also helped me make some sense of the conflicting evidence these new sources present us with. I could not have completed this book without her.

THE MYTH
OF PERSEPHONE

———•◦◆◦•———

M y grandfather thought of himself as something of a classicist, so it is not surprising that he opened his history of the township with an examination of its origins in Greek mythology. Rather than lean back on the cucumber frame of my own classical education, I have drawn freely from Dr. Goulding's summary of the Persephone myth in the preparation of this prologue.

According to the ancient Greeks, Persephone was the daughter of Demeter, the goddess of earth, agriculture, supply management, and the corn/soybean rotation. One day while picking daffodils beside the rippling waters of the Euthanasia River, on the Plain of Mysa, in ancient Eleusis, somewhere northwest of present-day Sarnia, the pretty young Persephone was startled by a rumble deep down in the earth. A great chasm opened at her feet, and out of the hole galloped two black horses with fiery eyes and hooves of flint that struck sparks from the rocks. The horses were pulling a chariot driven by Persephone's Uncle Hades. Before the girl had a chance to say "Hi, Uncle Hades. Mom's out in the garden. I'll put the kettle on," Hades reached out with one arm, scooped her up, and vanished back into the earth.

Demeter heard a scream and rushed to the Plain of Mysa, but found nothing. She knew her daughter had been abducted, and she went on a search that lasted nine days and covered the whole of the earth. During this time, she forbade the trees to yield fruit or the herbs to grow, so that the earth became sterile and the race of men stood in danger of extinction. But of her daughter she could find no trace.

Now, it's hard to pull off earthquake abductions in a small community without somebody noticing something. Persephone's scream was also heard by one of the locals, Eubuleus, a swineherd who was moving his pigs across the Plain of Mysa. He too saw the hole in the ground, and the next thing he knew, all of his pigs had vanished. Eubuleus was a man of very few words who didn't get out much. Nine days later, at the end of Demeter's search, he was down in the local diner complaining that it was just his luck that the price of pigs had tripled when he was fresh out of them. This prompted his brother Triptolemus to ask what had happened to his pigs. Eubuleus told him about the hole in the ground.

"Did you see anything suspicious? A truck, maybe, or a stock trailer?"

Eubuleus said that, come to think of it, he had seen a guy in black with his head shrouded, galloping by in a chariot. He had one arm around a woman and she was screaming her head off.

This news pretty much emptied out the diner. Triptolemus went straight to Demeter with a solid lead on what had happened to her daughter.

Demeter went to Zeus, who was her husband although they weren't living together at that point because Zeus liked dressing up as a horse and chasing her around Olympus. Demeter demanded that Hades return Persephone immediately. This put Zeus in a difficult position with his brother, and he put the case to Hades thus: "If you do not restore Persephone to Demeter, we are all undone. She's been gone nine days and already the place looks like the Sudbury Basin."

Zeus promised Demeter that her daughter would be returned to her on the condition that she had not tasted any food of the dead while in the underworld. When Persephone heard this news she was filled with joy, because she had refused to eat so much as a crust of bread since her abduction. But just as Hades was helping Persephone into the chariot of Hermes for her trip back up to the earth, his gardener whispered in his ear that he had seen Persephone eating a pomegranate in the orchard. She had eaten seven seeds from that fruit. Hades smiled, stuck the gardener in the back seat as a witness, and zipped up to Olympus, where the happy reunion of mother and daughter took place.

Then Hades brought up the pomegranate business and Demeter grew more dejected than ever and announced that she would never smile again. She said that as far as she was concerned, the branches of all the trees would be as productive as hoe handles and the race of men could suck rocks before she would see another twig sprout in the land. Finally, a compromise was reached. They agreed that Persephone must divide her time between the underworld and the world above: nine months of the year in the upper world with Demeter, three months below with Hades. Each spring, when the first shoots appear in the furrows, Persephone escapes from the nether regions and makes her way towards the sky. For a time, the winds are warm and the weather is lovely, but when fall seeding comes around, Persephone returns to the shades. Winter grips the land for as long as Persephone and Demeter are separated.*

The cult of Demeter and Persephone enjoyed great popularity and endured through the centuries. The essential elements of the myth were handed down to us through the Celts, who preserved many of the rituals in an oral tradition of do's and don'ts related to food production and the natural world. The Demeter cult dovetailed nicely with the Celts' belief in the evil eye and their preference for songs in a minor key about various members of the immediate family washing up on shore after a day's fishing. The ancient Greek and Celtic traditions find a common ground in their distrust of the New Testament notion that life should be joyful.

Demeter had a very short temper, and most residents of the ancient world had received one of her backhands, including several players in the Persephone abduction episode. She pushed the gardener of Hades into a hole that she covered with a large rock. When Hercules moved the rock, she changed the gardener into a barn owl. She punished the people of Phytopthora for not showing her greater hospitality during her wanderings. They were never allowed to grow soybeans again and might have disappeared altogether if they hadn't turned to sod farming

---

* The lengths of time vary depending on the source. According to Canadian classical scholars, Persephone spends nine months in the underworld, because it's warmer there and the dollar goes farther than it does in Florida. She comes to the Canadian Shield for three months each year, giving us a growing season that is suitable for the cultivation of Scotch thistle, burdock, a great variety of lichens and moss, and of course turnips and zucchini.

and subdivisions. On the other hand, she could be very generous. To reward him for telling her about Persephone's abduction, she taught Triptolemus the arts of agriculture, which had, up to that point, been a secret known by women only. She sent Triptolemus around the earth teaching these mysteries to other peoples, which made him the first agricultural representative in the Extension Branch of the Ministry of Agriculture. There are many odd prohibitions in farming that owe their origin to some peculiar dictate of Demeter. Farmers are careful never to plow down snow, or cut down sacred groves, or fail to turn up at the Eleusian Mysteries in early fall (the Outdoor Farm Show) or the Lesser Mysteries in early spring (John Deere Dealer Days).

The essential point of the Demeter-and-Persephone myth is that farming is a very tricky business, and you have to hold your mouth right to get through a season without being whacked by some natural calamity. There is only one certainty. Every spring, Persephone rises to the earth and the land becomes warm and lovely. In the fall she returns to the underworld, the price of wheat drops like a stone, and you'd better have six bush cords of maple stacked up against the side of the house.

Persephone's name comes from the Greek word meaning "ravaged, ruined or repeatedly abducted," which makes it a very apt name to give a township that has been ravished so often by generations of buccaneers and swindlers. Whatever freshness and beauty she brings to the world, you have to remember that Persephone also carries the titles Queen of Darkness and Nymph of the River of Hell. She owns a very fierce dog named Cerberus, who was the original junkyard dog. Persephone can turn on you, too.

5

This Ottawa statue purports to portray Samuel Champlain taking a sighting with his faithful astrolabe. However, the great explorer is holding the thing upside down. More likely the sculptor has caught him in the act of tossing it into the woods near Arnprior, Ontario, in the spring of 1613. A farmboy found it 254 years later.

Chapter 1

PERSEPHONE THROUGH THE AGES
3,000 MILLION BCE TO 1831

————◆•◆•◆————

The trick about writing the history of a place like
Persephone is knowing where to start. My grandfather
chose geography as his jumping-off point, which is traditional in a country with so much of it. After half an hour
twiddling my pencil on the top of the bar, I decided that
Grandfather probably had a good reason to start where he
did: no archaeologist has made his reputation examining
the life of ancient cities in Persephone; no papyrus scrolls
have been found for a scholar of the humanities to ponder.
Geography it is.

Canada is often portrayed as a wasteland of ice, snow, and
large rocks. It comes as a surprise to many visitors to learn
that almost 3 percent of the land mass does have topsoil and
can support some form of human activity. Very little of that
topsoil settled on Persephone, through no fault of its own.

The land mass of Canada takes roughly the shape of a
dinner plate lying face down and propped up slightly on its
left edge. The land rises slowly from the Atlantic seaboard

and crosses a bump of inland mountains before proceeding uphill, upwind, and upstream to a great inland plateau. These plains, in turn, rise until they encounter a final bump of mountains and then descend sharply to the Pacific Ocean. The five Great Lakes, the largest source of fresh water on the planet, appear at the one-third mark on this journey. Three of these lakes frame the long pointed boot of southern Ontario, which is home to most of the industrial, financial, and food-producing clout of the country. This boot sheathes the foot that kicks the Canadian economy (and most of the other provinces) to life. A narrow strip of habitation, no more than forty miles wide in places, extends from a point just east of Toronto to the American border at Detroit and holds the greatest concentration of the nation's population and prosperity.

About two hours north of Toronto, however, the well-kept dairy farms with their tall silos and fields of tasselled corn gradually give way to rolling hills and hardwood forests. North of Highway 13, the landscape changes abruptly to rugged treeless hills and valleys choked with cedar swamps.* Feldspar outcroppings appear in the pastures and skinny cows cling to the sides of eroded sand slopes. Weather-beaten pickup trucks wend their way along narrow dirt roads, trailing plumes of dust. Red brick farmhouses perch on the exposed heights, surrounded by dilapidated cedar-shingled outbuildings and piles of rusted farm equipment.

It is here, in the transition zone between the populous and prosperous heartland of southern Ontario and the

---

* Highway 13 was this road's pre-restructuring number, and the one most Persephone residents use to refer to it. Its formal name is now County Road 113, for reasons known only to God and the Ministry of Transportation. But when you use this new number, no one knows what road you are talking about.

Canadian Shield (a wilderness of granite rocks and stunted vegetation that stretches north in an unbroken sweep to the Arctic seas), that you find Persephone Township.

The future Persephone Township began to take on its current geographic shape during the Pre-Cambrian era, about 2,500 to 3,000 million years ago. This is a difficult period of time to hold in the imagination unless you've sat through a meeting of the Hillview Township Council. Geology was one of Dr. Goulding's hobbies, and he did his best to summarize the cooling of the Permian seas and the advance and retreat of great glaciers. After glancing through my grandfather's opening chapter, which is entirely devoted to the geological prehistory of Persephone, I decided that the only humane course of action for the reader would be to touch briefly on those significant events in geological time that created the township's present-day topography.

A distinct bedrock formation and a tumult of glacial activity determined the general shape of Persephone. The Great Rift is a fault line that caused the collapse of a long section of the township on an axis northwest to southeast. The spillway of the retreating glaciers carved a notch in the rift, creating a pathway for the Boyne and Pine Rivers.

I can't be sure if my grandfather was serious when he wrote: "Geology and history combine to place Larkspur at the centre of many stirring moments in the history of Canada. At various times, it has served as the spillway of the Wisconsin Glacier, an ancient campground on the trade route to the Northwest, and the first European settlement west of the Petunia River. Although sadly declined, it still serves as a crossroads in the best sense, as the emotional nucleus of a human community."

"Stirring" is not a word I would have used to describe an event as drawn out as the draining of old Lake Wisconsin, but then some people up here get excited about the return of the bay-breasted warbler every spring. The most stirring thing I have seen in Larkspur since I came back here was a deer that jumped through the plate glass window of MacKelvey's hardware store and ran out through the back. It was the only customer they had that afternoon.

As Dr. Goulding so exhaustingly explains, at least four glaciers locked the township in their grip in prehistoric times, scouring the earth down to bedrock like a giant SOS pad and grinding mountain ranges into gravel. When the last glacier retreated about twelve thousand years ago, its meltwaters spewed rocks and ice cubes across a wide area, leaving the land covered with millions of fist-size stones that the farmers today call "Irish confetti." The township is also famous for its "erratics" (some of whom will turn up later). In geological terms, an erratic is a very large rock that has been carried a great distance by the ice sheets and deposited someplace awkward, like where you were planning to put a garden.

Then there are the "leverites." A leverite is a big pink granite rock about the size of a piano – and you "leave 'er right there," unless you can sell it to the government, which is what people did in Persephone in the 1880s. It is a little-known fact that the exterior of the Provincial Legislative Building in Toronto is constructed entirely of very expensive pink leverites from the Corrie McQuarrie Quarries just east of Hollyhock.*

---

* Corrie McQuarrie also furnished the stones for the County Court House, the County Fire Hall, and the County Jail, where he spent his declining years serving a term for bid-rigging and bribery of government officials. Many residents of the township relied on McQuarrie Quarries stones as fitting markers for their final resting places in the Larkspur, Hollyhock, and Lavender cemeteries until the pit was finally closed in 1972.

Despite millions of years of glaciation, striation, sedimentation, and fermentation, the Great Rift is still plainly visible. Just north of Larkspur, it turns and runs more or less parallel to the lakeshore as it heads west.* As you approach Persephone from the east, the rift's most striking feature is a section of the escarpment where the granite is exposed. This granite face is now known as Pipesmoke Mountain. The highland (or horst), which stretches away to the west from the cliff edge, is fully three hundred feet higher than the valley floor (or graben), which extends from the southeast corner of the township and provides a pathway for the Pine and Petunia Rivers down to the shale beach at Port Petunia.

The soils of the valley floor are fertile black loams that today support many field and orchard crops. The soils of the highlands are a horst of a different colour. They are composed mostly of glacial till, discarded horseshoes, and old licence plates and possess excellent polishing properties. After a day of slicing through the glacial till on the heights around Hall's Corners, you can see your reflection clearly on even the oldest mouldboard. After three days of plowing, however, you can see right through the mouldboard itself, and you have to get a new plow. Tillage of highland soils has lost popularity over the last century and most of the land is now pastured by cattle and sheep – and very few of those. Visitors from abroad remark how similar the highland landscape of Persephone is to some parts of Afghanistan.

* The geological rift should not be confused with the religious rift that separated the Irish Catholics and Protestants, or the political rift that separated the Conservatives from the Liberals. Nor should it be mistaken for the lesser rifts that divided the school board, the church groups, the fair board, and many marriages nor for the deep rift that still afflicts the Larkspur Gun Club.

A distinctive feature of the highlands is the drumlin, a type of hill created by the retreat of a glacier. It is an oval-shaped mound of boulder clay that looks a bit like a snow-drift and covers an area roughly the size of a city block. It has an abrupt southern slope and a northern slope that is more gradual. Each drumlin will support up to two sheep at a time, provided the sheep are fond of Scotch thistles. The north slope is the last surface to lose its cover of snow in the springtime and the first to be hit by frost in the fall. Farmers usually drive off the sharp end of a drumlin at some point in their careers, suffering permanent injury. Cedar fence posts rot quickly in its sand, which is why most drumlin fences lie flat on the ground, making them useless for restricting the movement of livestock.

A geologist who was trying to explain why the life expectancy of the Irish had not kept pace with the general advances in Europe over the preceding five hundred years first identified the drumlin in Northern Ireland in 1866.* His research indicated that drumlins were part of the problem. When the Irish moved to Canada they instinctively moved to the nearest drumlin, cleared it of all trees, and settled down to the hand-to-mouth existence they were accustomed to. Many of Persephone's families can trace their origins to a particular set of drumlins for which they feel a fierce and inexplicable affection. For example, you might hear one of them say, "I'm assessed for a hundred acres, but I've got nearly twice that. It's all up on its edge and the cows can pasture both sides."

Drumlin farmers are proud, clannish, and contemptuous

---

* The reader may be interested to consult the work of P. McBride, "Which Came First: the Irish or the Drumlin?" *Royal Geographic Conference Proceedings*, Vol. 27 (1870). I am informed by reliable sources that it is a fascinating essay.

of anyone who farms in the "flats" of the Petunia and Pine River Valleys. Most of them limp. They firmly believe that farmers who grow crops in topsoil are cheating. Anybody can do that. It takes great skill to coax a crop of spring grain out of the north slope of a drumlin, as they are happy to remind anyone who slips into a booth in the Red Hen Restaurant in Larkspur today. In modern times, the highest and best use of a drumlin appears to be a golf course.

If you look at a climate and soil map for southern Ontario, you will see a small circular zone marked 4a. This area encloses the highlands of the township, giving it a climate and growing conditions very much like the south of France during July and August. For the rest of the year it is more like Churchill, Manitoba. In the narrow strip of the Pine River Valley down to Port Petunia, the designation is a slightly more forgiving 5b. There is considerable evidence that the climate in Persephone Township has been warming steadily for several centuries.

Climatic data before 1833 are largely unavailable, so I have been forced to speculate about the rate of this warming trend, assuming that the low point was reached about fifty thousand years ago when the ice pack over Persephone was probably about a mile and a quarter thick. The progress towards temperateness would appear to have been quite slow, given the references in the seventy-three volumes of the seventeenth-century *Jesuit Relations* to the six-month winters and Champlain's claim in his doorstopping *Voyages* that "no white man has ever been quite so cold for so long a period of time." Over the Internet I was able to contact a Jesuit who had read some of this material, and he was able to direct me to certain relevant passages. Of course, the French spent the winters here in houses with walls of birchbark and went about in bare feet. Champlain himself passed the entire winter with nothing between him and the ground but a "thin Indian maid."*

Father Gauloise, one of the early Récollet priests ministering to the Petun Indian village of Tationtinate (which translates as "close to schools and transit"), reported that ice had formed on the lake before Christmas in 1636. On New Year's Day it was thick enough for him to walk across the narrow channel between the site of present-day Port Petunia and the nearby Hawk and Hatchling Islands for a week of ice fishing. He returned with a bad cold and a case of hemorrhoids from sitting on the ice that made his later rough treatment as a captive of the Iroquois seem like a picnic by comparison. Today ice seldom forms on the bay until late February and in some years not at all. The ice-fishing industry has moved far to the north, removing yet another source of much-needed income from the community but considerably reducing the waiting time for elective surgery at the Port Petunia Marine Hospital.

However cold the winters may have been, it is also clear that the summers could be brutally hot.† The fossil record shows evidence of mussels cooked in their own shells, and tree rings during certain periods are closer together than the eyeballs of a Ministry of Transportation truck inspector, which indicates that at times trees almost stopped growing entirely. Today the last serious frosts occur in early June, and freezing temperatures do not resume until the second week of September. Annual rainfall varies between zero

* *Les Voyages de la Nouvelle France occidentale, dicte Canada: faits par le Sr de Champlain* . . . (Paris: Louis Sevestre, 1632). The translation is mine.

† There is other evidence of high heat and humidity. Étienne Brûlé, the notorious French explorer, guide, and early *coureur de bois*, came to an untimely end because of excessively high temperatures at a Huron banquet he attended in 1633.

and fifty inches. Much of this precipitation comes in the form of snow. Fifty-year storms occur about once every three or four years, and tornado sightings have been recorded at least once every season since 1834. According to my grandfather: "The residents of Persephone never lack for a subject of conversation as long as the weather presents such opportunities for diversity and astonishment."

The prevailing winds in Persephone blow steadily enough that when they stop, cattle fall over. The Westerlies sweep in off the lake at high speed and collide with the drumlins of the highlands, the first and only obstruction they have encountered on the trip east from Winnipeg. Botanists have identified a local subspecies of conifer that locals call the Persephone pine. It has branches only on the east side.

The winds gave housebound pioneer women of the area the peculiar glassy-eyed stare that is recorded in many old photographs. Like the mistral in Provence and the Santa Ana in California, the Persephone Westerlies have inspired much poetry, but none of it has been published.* The wind was used successfully as a legal defence in the murder trial of the Widow McClay (*R. v. McClay*, 1923). After three months of listening to the windows rattle in the northwest gales, her husband greeted her at the dinner hour with the question, "Say, did you feel that breeze out there?" She bludgeoned him to death with a chunk of cordwood. Mrs. McClay was granted an absolute discharge on the condition that she move into town.

Despite the challenges of wind and winter, an assortment of hardy flora and fauna can be observed in Persephone. The

---

* Probably because of its excessive dependence on profanity. For example: "Every day, from off the Bay the —— wind doth Blow, / And what the —— a man's to do, I —— do not know . . ." – Anon.

flower on the township coat of arms is the pretty columbine, an exotic drooping plant of crimson and yellow that grows everywhere in Persephone and the neighbouring townships. It is an ancient symbol of peace. It is also a stimulant with powerful narcotic properties. Plantings of columbine can now be found throughout the area.

Most indigenous tree species except the Persephone pine were cleared off in the days of early settlement and were replaced during the reforestation effort of the 1930s with spruce, pine, cedar, chokecherries, and dogwood. Not many houses are built out of dogwood these days (although some farmers up in the highlands still repair fences with grapevines and large burdocks), and the lumber industry is pretty much extinct. However, the eastern slope of Pipesmoke Mountain and the Pine and Petunia River Valleys have been designated by the United Nations as a World Biosphere Reserve. Many exotic and significant plant and animal species can be found here, including the zebra mussel, the purple loosestrife, the lamprey eel, the stinging nettle, poison oak, and the Rift rattlesnake, which is basically harmless if you're within ten minutes of a hospital.

In the second week of my stay in Larkspur I found myself trapped in yet another confab with the reeve and his entourage in a haze of bacon and cigarette smoke in the Red Hen Restaurant. After a decent interval I excused myself and went outside for a stroll along the Pine. The sun came out and some raucous red-winged blackbirds scolded me from the scrubby saplings that grow along the riverbank. As I made my way along the fishing path that follows the river, the birds were replaced by two large flies that circled my head, trying to take a piece out of my ear. I headed uphill to escape them along a little lane that winds up the side of Hall's Hill. After a vigorous climb I reached the summit and was rewarded with an impressive view of the lake away to the north and, in the distance, the great Hawk Island with her little Hatchling Islands in a row behind her in the blue-green water. But I'd walked long enough. It was time to return to the reeve in his smoke-filled den.

I was about to turn back down the path when I heard voices. I noticed a group of middle-aged types in Bermuda shorts a little way off, just sitting down to a picnic lunch on the crest of the hill. One of them was a pleasant red-haired woman about my age with an outdoor freshness about her. She mopped her freckled brow with a napkin from their hamper and explained that they were a band of volunteers with the Watershed Biological Trust who were releasing Rift rattlesnakes back into the wild in an attempt to re-establish a small core population of this indigenous species. According to the geodetic survey, she informed me, Hall's Hill is the second-highest point in southern Ontario.* I would have stayed for lunch, but I wasn't sure which hamper had the snakes in it.

The second-oldest man-made structure in the county is the assemblage of ancient stone fishing weirs at the narrows between Hawk Island and the mainland near Port Petunia, which were built by the township's first inhabitants nearly four thousand years ago. (The oldest structure, of course, is the Commercial Hotel, in Larkspur, which must be at least five thousand years old.)

We don't know who those first inhabitants were, but it's more than likely they were Conservatives. A young boy

---

* The volunteer in question was Ms. Doreen Cameron. I happened to mention my writing project and the difficulty I was having in documenting some of the more elusive episodes in Persephone's early years. She kindly offered to assist me in my researches.

picking stones in a cornfield near Larkspur in April 1965 discovered the earliest evidence of human beings in Persephone. He turned up a fishing spear that showed some similarity in craftsmanship to the Ohio flints of the Paleo-Indian era, about six to eight thousand years ago. The boy found that the spear worked as well in the modern age as it had in prehistoric times, and it was confiscated from him by a conservation officer along with five out-of-season rainbow trout. It now rests in the restored railway station museum in Port Petunia.

In the seventeenth century, the slope below Pipesmoke Mountain was the home of the Petun Indians, sometimes called the Tobacco Nation of the Huron people. The Petuns spent their days hunting, fishing, growing their own smoking material, and cultivating the three sisters: corn, squash, and runner beans. Nearly five hundred years later, the residents of Persephone Township still hunt and fish through the area. They too grow their own smoking material and, if weather permits, they do a little farming on the side.

The first contact between Europeans and the indigenous population did not take place until 1615, when Étienne Brûlé guided his old friend Samuel de Champlain to the land of the Petuns.* That summer, several of Champlain's men drowned when a canoe overturned in the rapids of the

---

* It is becoming increasingly obvious to present-day historians that Champlain was lost pretty much from the day he left his veranda in Brouage on the coast of Brittany, France, in 1603 until Christmas Day in 1635, when he died in Quebec City. He left six volumes of travel notes that contain only one reference to any recognizable physical landform west of Montreal, that being the Lachine Rapids, which had been marked on a map previously by Jacques Cartier, who believed he had found the Yangtze River. Historians say there is some evidence that Champlain spent the winter of 1615-16 in Persephone Township, but then again it could have been the area near what is now Chatham,

Ottawa River, a tragic moment that was turned to great advantage by this ingenious explorer. Champlain noted that his Indian guides popped to the surface and were rescued, which prompted him to order his men to dispense with the conventional fifty-pound steel breastplate and helmet, the leather jerkin, and steel-toed boots in favour of doeskin underpants and primitive life preservers made of short cedar planks and rawhide. Not only did this innovation result in a remarkable increase in life expectancy, it proved to be an enormous relief to the French in coping with the brutal summer heat that Champlain frequently complained of in his journal. In another bold move, Champlain also banned horses from his canoes after this expedition, which cut travelling time even further.

Pipesmoke Mountain gained its name from the tobacco haze that hung over its ridges in the dead of late summer in the time of the Jesuits. Father Gauloise, writing in the *Jesuit Relation* of 1643, mentions "the delicate play of sunlight and cloud along the hills on the western horizon, presenting a hazy aura, which is pleasing to the eye but is

---

Ontario, or the Finger Lakes district in New York State. By this time, he had long since thrown away his astrolabe and compass and was running bare-assed through the forest with his Indian friends. He did emerge from time to time over the next decade to ask for money from home, or to report some fresh quarrel he had started with the tribes to the south.

Champlain handed down to us very detailed accounts of his life with the people he called Indians, who clearly enjoyed his company and were happy to take him anywhere he wanted to go, which wasn't anywhere in particular. His employers often wrote to him asking for news of gold, northwest passages, fountains of youth, and so forth, but they went to their graves without satisfaction. It is an ironic footnote to his career that Champlain's grave and headstone have been misplaced. In death, as in life, his whereabouts are unknown.

offensive to the nostrils." The cleric was coming into contact for the first time with a tribe who had a serious smoking habit. The name Petun comes from the Huron word meaning "short of breath," and the Petun word Nottawasaga means "land of the morning cough."

Champlain was much taken with the area and named it Huronie, or Huronia, in honour of his guides, the Hurons, then acting as middlemen between the French and other tribes of what is now southern Ontario. In his blundering Eurocentric white male way, he failed to realize that the area already had a name, which was Petunia. The misapprehension continued for two more centuries and was only partially corrected with the naming of Port Petunia in 1852, which by that time carried the later Ojibway name of Oh-ke-won-do-say-mee (translation: "Why do you want to live down there with all those bugs?"). Then it was the Ojibway's turn to be offended.

In spite of some grumbling about the names, the Indian tribes coexisted quite peacefully. The Jesuit mission among the Petun met with limited success. After thirty years living among the native people, Father Gauloise could not document a single case of a successful Christian conversion. In 1649, the Iroquois passed a non-smoking bylaw, which upset the Petun nation and triggered the Tobacco Wars. The Iroquois drove the Petuns, the Hurons, and the French missionaries out of the area altogether, and a Dark Age began that lasted for more than a century.

Although the Jesuits recounted stories of savage battles between the Iroquois and the Petuns, with great loss of life on both sides, these are not first-hand accounts and cannot be relied on. One theory holds that the Jesuits were witnessing the quarter-final playoffs of the regional lacrosse season and didn't realize that the people being carried off the field were having fun and would probably recover from their injuries.

You have to remember the wide gulf that existed between these two great cultures, the European and the North American, the barriers of language and custom, theology and morality. Some of the Jesuit accounts of these "battles" were written by the abbé back in Quebec City four hundred miles away, and only after the bones of several of his missionaries had been delivered in a basket, with a birchbark note saying, "Please return the basket." This goes a long way towards explaining why one incident of 1649 in the village of Etharita is described in the *Jesuit Relations* by a certain Father Gitane as "a bloody massacre by the Iroquois" but comes down to us in the oral tradition of the Iroquois nation merely as "a solid hitting game."

After the departure of the Petuns, no settled human habitation occurred in Persephone Township for 150 years. The Iroquois, although ahead on points, never populated the area with any enthusiasm. They came in the fall of the year for an annual moose hunt and in the spring to fish for trout. The Ojibway tribes of the northern forests gradually spread down into the area during the 1700s, hunting and fishing the woods, lakes, and streams for the Hudson's Bay Company until they were emptier than the hills of Tuscany on the second day of the shooting season. These are the people who welcomed the vanguard of European settlement that arrived in the area in the early 1800s.

Although no portraits of Alexander MacNabb survive, he is said to have borne an uncanny resemblance to his cousin Archibald McNab (above) of Perth, Ontario, who claimed to be the thirteenth Laird of McNab and was the cousin of Ontario premier Allan Napier MacNab. All of them, of course, spelled their last names differently.

Chapter 2

WHO WAS FIRST?

1831 TO 1836

———————•◦◆◦•———————

When Grandfather sat down to write his history of
Persephone, he could speak to quite a few people
who'd been around for many of the events he was
chronicling. A good thing, because the documentary record
was pretty thin, with most documents still residing in
private hands. So he had to rely more on oral than on
written history. Which undoubtedly explains a number of
discrepancies between his version and the facts.

But he and I can agree that the story of European settlement of the area north of the town of York began during the
War of 1812-14. The naval commander on Lake Ontario,
Sir James Yeo, had been an officer under Horatio Nelson
but doesn't seem to have picked up any of the admiral's fighting habits. Yeo loved to build ships but he was terrified of
risking them in battle. When the Americans built a navy that
rivalled his, Sir James looked for a means of retreat – a
tricky concept in a lake closed off by Niagara Falls at one
end and by the impassable rapids of the St. Lawrence River

at the other. Undeterred, he devised an ingenious scheme to dismantle his ships plank by plank and carry them overland to Georgian Bay. He began construction of an extension to Lieutenant-Governor John Graves Simcoe's military road, Yonge Street, which had made it only as far as the southern-most bay of Lake Simcoe. The extension would continue this road all the way to Penetanguishene Harbour at the south-eastern tip of Georgian Bay.

One of the more endearing tales my grandfather recounts about this "epic feat of engineering" involved Admiral Richard Kempenfeldt, an officer famous for reforming the Royal Navy's flag-signalling system. It seems that one day in 1782, Admiral Kempenfeldt was supervising the repair at sea of his flagship, *Royal George*, which had been careened at a sharp angle in order to expose part of the hull. When a cutter pulled alongside and unloaded three hundred casks of rum into the hold over the low side, the flagship promptly rolled over and sank with the rum and the admiral in it. There was considerable loss of life in the sinking of the *Royal George*, but it was the loss of three hundred casks of rum that lodged deep in the memory of the British military man. Thirty years later, when the soldiers building the road to Penetanguishene learned that their rum rations had gone down in a gale on Lake Ontario, they named their base camp Kempenfeldt in the admiral's memory. He lives on to this day through the Lake Simcoe bay that bears his name. The village of Kempenfeldt has not been so fortunate, having vanished completely from contemporary maps.* But until the coming of the railway in the 1850s, the village was

---

* A recent archaeological dig in the area has unearthed a large number of rakes that early road builders used to lean on while waiting for someone to tell them what to do.

an important staging point for incoming settlement, with a post office, a log court house, a jail, and a barracks for the local militia.

In the absence of the rum, the road extension to Penetanguishene was completed in 1815, two years ahead of the schedule estimated on the colonial government road signs for the project. After the road finally punched through to the pink granite boulders of Penetanguishene Harbour, Sir James Yeo made the trip north and decided that the only disadvantage of his escape route was that it gave away the direction of his retreat. So he hatched plans for yet another road, this one going west from Kempenfeldt into an as yet unsurveyed wilderness, "to confuse the enemy and oblige them to divide their forces." The only ones to be confused by this strategy were the British themselves. For the next fifteen years the New Military Road existed solely as a dotted line on admiralty maps of British North America. In the meantime, lots on either side of the military road between Kempenfeldt and Penetanguishene were parcelled out to half-pay officers and soldiers from Wellington's army. As a result, it soon became known as the Fortunes of War Road.

In the 1820s, settlement of the lands north of York proceeded very slowly and did not venture far from this single rough track. There were encouragements to new settlers in the form of land grants. But few were willing to strike out into the lonely wilderness so far from the comforts of civilization. The forest west of Kempenfeldt was dense bush extending mile after mile across poorly drained, sandy soil dotted with impassable swamps.

The colonial authorities often chose names for new townships to remind settlers of home and to downplay the shortcomings of the Canadian climate and soil. Such was the case with the naming of Persephone. One day in the summer of 1831, Sir John Colborne, lieutenant-governor of Upper Canada, was about to leave his office for the afternoon hunt when his aide-de-camp bustled in with some official papers for him to sign. These included an order-in-council creating three new townships in the remote bush four days' journey northwest of the town of York. The aide-de-camp asked him to suggest some possible township names, and Sir John promptly proposed three of his favourite hounds, Scrap, Luke, and Red.

The aide remarked deferentially that Sir John's superior, the British colonial secretary, Lord Goderich, had recently written to advise that the lands in Upper Canada might be made more attractive to settlers if their names hinted at some suitability for agriculture. Perhaps, Goderich had suggested, they could make use of those gods and goddesses in the Greek myths who symbolized the planting and the harvest.

"Bang on," cried Sir John. "Hang the dogs, we'll go with the Greeks."*

This set the two of them rummaging through the attics of their classical educations. Eventually, Sir John's aide came up with the Greek goddesses of agriculture and spring, Demeter and Persephone, but was stumped on the name for the god of the underworld. After an uncomfortable silence, Sir John said, "Pluto, wasn't it?"

"I believe that was his Roman counterpart, sir," replied his aide. "I can't recall the Greek. I would have to find my copy of the *Theogony* of Hesiod."

"Hang Hesiod, Pluto will have to do," said Sir John

---

* Sir John's dogs have been immortalized in the names of various townships across Ontario's cottage country.

impatiently as he scratched his signature on the documents. Then he bounded out the door, leapt onto his waiting horse, and galloped off to the hunt.

It is at this point in his chronicle that my grandfather introduces the first of the big names of Persephone's early years, Captain Charles Augustus Fortescue, who later came to be known as the Champlain of Hillhurst County.* Were it not for Captain Fortescue's exploits, Persephone Township would look very different today. When you compare it with the orderly grid pattern of the townships around it, you'll see what I mean. Persephone sits on a 30-degree tilt compared with the normal inclination of its neighbours, and its borders and roads do not line up with those of any of the surrounding townships. It would appear that this peculiarity represents a bold attempt by Fortescue to survey the area without reference to any previous surveyor's mark.†

For my purposes, namely the post-contact saga of Persephone, Captain Fortescue enters the record in 1831, the year he secured a commission to survey the area around the mouth of the Petunia River on Georgian Bay to prepare it for settlement. Given Fortescue's crowded curriculum vitae, which included distinguished service under the Duke of Wellington during the Peninsular War and a significant contribution to General Isaac Brock's victory at the Battle of Queenston Heights, it must have seemed to his employer, the commissioner of Crown lands at York, that he was just the man for the job of bringing order to an unkempt wilderness. Time and again in his long and event-filled

---

* Hillhurst County includes the three townships Fortescue surveyed in the 1830s, Persephone, Demeter, and Pluto.

† This is known in surveyors' language as "an uncontrolled traverse from an unknown point, performed by a deviant while disoriented."

career, Fortescue had proved to be a man who understood the value of a straight line.*

Fortescue's commission was simple: "Lay out the Persephone farms in lots of One Hundred Acres, each lot to be located by Astronomical Course and Variation." For this work, he was to be paid 15 shillings; his chief chain-bearer 5 shillings; seven axemen 3 shillings each; and three strong backs to do the heavy lifting, 2 shillings each. He selected as his chief chain-bearer an old friend from the mess tents of Fort York, Terence Lynch, and for the rest of the crew he drew a sieve through the taverns on Yonge Street.

---

* Charles Augustus Fortescue did not live to write his autobiography, but he was a man of opportunity who had risen from humble origins in his native Cornwall, where he was born in 1791. His parents ran a lighthouse near Penzance but were so poor they could seldom afford to light the lamp. However, they were able to eke out a living clearing shipwreck debris from the shore. Charles tired of this arduous work and at the age of fourteen joined the British army. By 1808 he was serving in the Peninsular War against Napoleon. Military documents of the period state merely that he was either a cook or a cook's assistant. But Fortescue's later campaign literature in his race for a seat in the provincial legislature sheds considerably more light on a remarkable military career. Perhaps through modesty, he did not see fit to reveal until then that he had risen rapidly through the ranks on merit alone to become first a sergeant, then a lieutenant, and finally lieutenant general. He would have been a general except that the post was already filled by Arthur Wellesley, who was about to become the Duke of Wellington. So Fortescue had to content himself with being acting general while Wellington was in town. Together Wellington and Fortescue defeated many of Napoleon's finest marshals and enjoyed many happy times together. After a particularly clever thumping of Massena at the battle of Torres Vedras in 1810, Wellington began calling Fortescue "my beloved Charles," and Fortescue took to teasing Wellington as "Old Iron Pants." A remarkable accomplishment for a lad of nineteen, and difficult to believe, were it not for the fact that we have the authority of Fortescue's own account to verify it.

It was during the Peninsular War that Fortescue discovered his

In the only photograph of Captain Fortescue that survives, taken for his campaign for elected office in 1860, we see a man with the stamp of Wellington on him. He has the high forehead, beak nose, and thrust chin, but something about the eyes is wrong. They seem to focus about a thousand yards beyond the camera, producing an unsettling effect. Perhaps Dr. Goulding comes closest to explaining the personality of this man when he quotes several comments from elderly residents who knew Fortescue and remembered his "rabbit-like energy" and "firefly enthusiasms." Grandfather drew the conclusion that Fortescue was "quite mad."

———

lifelong love of charting unknown territory, especially during an attack by the enemy. He seems to have been able to think more strategically away from the sound of the guns. Throwing away his rifle and knapsack, he would take to the woods armed with nothing but a compass and a canteen. Eventually he would emerge, much to the surprise of the enemy, who, having tired of chasing him, then fell an easy prey to the disciplined British square, an infantry defensive position.

A grateful king and country dispatched Fortescue across the ocean to Kingston Harbour on Lake Ontario with a contingent of prisoners of war and deserters to help fight the new enemy, the Americans, in the War of 1812. Fortescue asked to be returned to the ranks to pursue his first love, the feeding of his brother officers in the army mess tent. From there he took ship for the fledgling town of York, there to join a small contingent of British regulars led by General Isaac Brock. Shortly after that he found himself at the foot of Queenston Heights, just as the American army began crossing the Niagara River to invade Canada. Seeing so many of the enemy massed on the opposite side of the river, Fortescue instinctively reverted to his Peninsular War tactics and again took to the woods. This time he shed his rifle and knapsack and unbuckled his sword, which allowed him to make better time than ever. The Indians who tried to follow him were amazed at his speed and agility and christened him "Runs with Rabbits" in a traditional ceremony, some time after the battle, at which they returned his sword to him.

The route Fortescue took between Niagara and Fort York was so straight that it was later adopted as a road by the military and later still by the provincial roads department as the Queen Elizabeth Way.

In the spring of 1831 Fortescue travelled north from York with his crew. When they arrived at Kempenfeldt, he was supposed to take a bearing from one of the markers on the road and strike off west into the wilderness. However, it was blackfly season and the men were already complaining, so he decided to come at his quarry from the lake. He pressed on along the Fortunes of War Road to Penetanguishene and set sail with his crew in a skiff, making his way along the bay and down to the mouth of the Petunia River. Here his boat and supplies were hurled onto a shale rock beach by a violent late-spring storm.* (Both skiff and supplies miraculously survived.) The Petunia River was in full torrent and the party camped on the beach for several days watching the churning brown waters roar past, carrying uprooted trees and the carcasses of moose and deer and tearing great chunks out of the riverbank.

We know today that Fortescue was the first European to explore the shale rock beach west of the present-day site of Port Petunia, which is considerably beyond the point to which Champlain may or may not have penetrated during his explorations of the area two hundred years earlier. While waiting for the river to subside, Fortescue happened on a place where the rocks had an oily sheen. When he placed several of these near the campfire's heat, a liquid we would now recognize as kerosene dripped down into the coals and burst into a smoky yellow flame. Although he made no mention of this discovery in his survey, he scribbled extensive notes in a leatherbound scrapbook that survives in a glass case in the main foyer of the Larkspur library.† In this

* This is the first documented fifty-year storm in Persephone.

† This scrapbook was the first of a series that Fortescue kept throughout his life. They are bound in calfskin and carry notes, sketches, maps, and various articles pressed between the pages.

book he drew a simple sketch of a boiler and ore chamber, a contraption that would sweat the kerosene out of these rocks. This sketch, which he labelled "The Extractor," bears a remarkable resemblance to the machine he would build twenty-five years later. But I'm getting ahead of my story.

After three days, the river was still in flood and Fortescue had no choice but to haul the skiff up on shore and head inland on foot. He led his party along the west bank of the Petunia River, hacking his way through the thick underbrush with the sword he had thrown away and then regained at Queenston Heights. Fighting blackflies and sunburn, the surveyors passed the point where the raging torrent of the Petunia was joined by the calm, clear waters of the Pine. In the early afternoon they reached the confluence of the Pine and a small tributary, the Boyne. Dr. Goulding captures the moment as if he were describing the landing of the pilgrims at Plymouth Rock.

The Captain called a halt and scrambled to the top of a rise into a clearing bright with blue flowers. A fresh breeze from the north fanned his face, giving him the first relief from the insects since leaving the shoreline. The granite face of the Great Rift towered above him and in the distance he could see the sun's dappling on the waters of the Bay. He shouted down to his crew that this would be the base camp for the survey of Persephone. While the men set up the tents and organized their equipment, their leader sat on a boulder in the middle of the clearing and made notes in his scrapbook. After careful sightings and meas-urements, he calculated that he was within a few miles of the place where Sir James Yeo's imaginary New Military Road petered out. He bent down to the blue flowers at his feet, plucked one, and held it to his nose. "Terry," he called to his chief chain-bearer, "what kind of flower do you suppose this is?"

"'Tis the henbane of the marsh, sir, the blue gentian of the bog that makes the cattle mad, the flower that maids call Larkspur."

"Then Larkspur it shall be," said Fortescue and made a notation on his map.

Larkspur
Township of Persephone
Overland by skiff and foot this day 25th June, 1831

With the help of the part-time archivist at the Larkspur library, I have been able to examine the captain's scrapbook in some detail. Opposite the drawing of the Extractor there is a spray of blue flowers pressed between the pages.

Nineteenth-century surveyors were not equipped with the sophisticated measuring devices of today. They marked lots with blazes on trees and wooden stakes. The builders who followed often had to move to one side or the other to avoid steep hills and rivers. To add to the confusion, the surveyors' chains grew longer with use. Nor were the surveyors themselves always sober. This is why some of today's farms in Persephone are 90 acres and some are 110, and the buyer is always warned that the figure given on the deed is "more or less" accurate. After a summer's work in the bush, Fortescue sent back a report that speaks for itself about the conditions he found in the wilderness.

25th October, 1831
Dear Sirs:

In obedience to your instructions of March last, I

have proceeded to the Survey of Persephone with the
Diligense commended to me by your Letter.

We are finally relieved of the Humidity and the
Affliction of the insects, but I must confess I know
not whether to trade such Conditions for the most
severe Blasts of Winter which now fall upon us. The
Task is done, and so I fear are my Crew. Four of
them have been confined to their Tents with Fever
this past week, despite my strict Instructions that
Fever was to be left in Penetang.

As for the prospects of Settlement, I woulde
advise that there is some Hindrance on account of the
Absence of Topsoil, the difficulty of ploughing
Limestone, the sheer impenetrability of the Forest,
the Ferocity of the Winters and a growing season that
furnishes more entertainments in the form of Hail,
Tempests and Sharp Frostes than the farmers at
home might witness in a Lifetime. Apart from this,
Conditions appear to be most Favourable. Settlers
should be advised that there is no shortage of Wild
Game, including the Weasel, the Skunk, the
Wolverine and a species of Large Cat that the Indians
call ppphhhtuii.

I am, Sir,

Your most obt. hbl. Srvt.

Capt. Charles Fortescue, District Land Surveyor

Much of what Fortescue had to say about the township as he found it in 1831 seems to be accurate. But the
surveyor deliberately overstated the obstacles to settlement in an attempt to play down the value of land in
Persephone until he was in a position to get control of it.

The highlands do present obvious challenges and the Petunia River Valley is dangerously prone to flooding. But there is a narrow strip of fertile plain along the west side of the Pine River below Larkspur that caught Fortescue's eye. On his original survey he named the entire plain King William's Marsh, although none of it was under water. He also did not refer to the burning rocks on the beach, which he would later name after himself.

Following a stormy return passage along the bay, the crew arrived in Penetanguishene to find the harbour already frozen. They dragged the skiff the last five miles across the ice and collapsed in the nearest tavern. Seven days later, Fortescue set off for York to file his report. Jolting along the snow-packed Fortunes of War Road in a horse-drawn mail sled with six other passengers, he had plenty of time to reflect on how he would present his findings to the authorities and make the best use of them for his own purposes.

Surveyors were often paid in land, and some eventually settled on their acreages to become farmers. But the real profits came from their manipulation of land purchases and the inside information they possessed about the choicest parcels. Fortescue was no farmer; his ambition was to secure fresh survey contracts and an appointment as a locator, the person who guided prospective pioneers into the township to their land grants.

A handful of government administrators, army officers, and clerics – known in the colony as the Family Compact – controlled all matters of settlement in Upper Canada in this period.* Every appointment went through the lieutenant-

---

* Control of the provincial government has been considerably streamlined since that time. Decision-making now rests in the hands of about three people: the premier, his speechwriter, and his pollster.

governor's office and passed under the sharp eye of the Reverend John Strachan, the leader of the Church of England in Upper Canada and the éminence grise in the vice-regal chambers.

I have reason to believe that Fortescue went to Strachan and persuaded him to support his applications in return for advice about which lands should be designated for the church under the clergy reserves system.* One-seventh of all new lands were set aside for the church. Strachan's son-in-law was the co-commissioner of the privately held Canada Company, then busy purchasing large tracts of the Ontario wilderness from the government and selling lots to settlers. With Fortescue looking over his shoulder and giving advice, Strachan would have had a distinct advantage in selecting the best lands for the church and for his son-in-law, which is exactly what happened. Strachan also seems to have recommended Fortescue as a locator for the Crown. And it was Fortescue who resurrected Sir James Yeo's imaginary escape route, the line on the Admiralty map that led into the heart of Persephone to Larkspur.

By the spring of 1832, Captain Fortescue and his crew were once again cutting their way into the bush, this time striking west from Kempenfeldt, having been awarded the contract to survey and build the New Military Road along Yeo's planned route. At the end of the year, they reached the Petunia River, where they began construction of a pontoon bridge. The next spring, Fortescue climbed a rudimentary wooden tower built for this purpose and took a sighting on the granite cliff he had seen at close range the previous spring, now clearly visible in the distance. Then

---

* Fortescue's estate included a single place setting of Strachan's silverware, which indicates he had dinner with the cleric about this time.

he ordered his crew off into the bush to mark the trail west. "The virgin forest now parted," writes Dr. Goulding, "Persephone lay soft and verdant and ready for her next assignation with history."

The next name on her dance card was Alexander MacNabb, who towers over Persephone's early years like the mighty wall of Pipesmoke Mountain. Nearly every contemporary source carries at least some reference to his building projects, his autocratic dealings with the settlers, his stinginess, and his fierce temper. His name is better known to the schoolchildren of the community than that of our first prime minister. But there is very little physical evidence that he actually existed. He left no heirs and no papers, and the land records have little to say. Even my grandfather's comprehensive work skips over the details of MacNabb's life.* To reconstruct the major events of his career I have relied mostly on local sources unknown to Dr.

---

* Alexander Lachlan MacNabb traced his descent from one of the most impoverished aristocratic families of Scotland. The first Laird MacNabb is alternately described in various histories of the Outer Hebrides as "an abbot," or "the son of an abbot," or "the son of a [illegible]." Between the twelfth and fifteenth centuries the first ten lairds built their positions as community leaders on the twin pillars of the church and commerce. Through a combination of shrewd dealings and brute force, they came to master the four main industries that fuelled the Glen Islet economy: sheep rustling, smuggling, piracy, and taxing the peasants without mercy. The MacNabb formula for success was simple: maintain a small private army, take what you want from all who pass through your territory, then kill them.

The history of the MacNabb family is one long tale of knife fights, stolen cattle, and treacherous dinner parties that makes very repetitive reading. By the seventeenth century, they held most of the land on Glen Islet and had a vast number of serfs and tenant farmers working for them. In 1734, Donald the Bold founded the first distillery on Glen Islet and the family fortunes quickly ran downhill. Strong drink, strange women, and life in drafty castles took its toll on the MacNabb genetics.

Goulding: diaries of those who knew him and correspondence out of the settlement. I consulted the MacNabb genealogical Website but found its keepers cannot agree on a single fact before 1900, including the spelling of their own name.*

The MacNabb who figures in the Persephone story was born on Glen Islet in 1781 and grew to be a tall strapping young man with a wide face and huge eyebrows. He

———•———

Donald spent a lot of time racing horses on the Continent and died in the arms of a famous courtesan in Paris at the age of thirty-seven. His son, Duguid the Deviant, mortgaged his properties heavily, took up racing greyhounds, and died in the arms of his gamekeeper. The title passed to his nephew, Donald the Soft, who took out second mortgages at ruinous terms, raced pigeons, and died in the arms of a sheep.

In the year 1788, someone reported that the local horses were being fed more oats per pound of body weight than were the local peasants. This revelation provoked a violent uprising, led by the Camerons, which became known as the Glen Islet Mutiny. It was ruthlessly crushed by the MacNabbs. After the mutiny, anyone who had the financial means to escape Glen Islet did so.

The late eighteenth century was a time of distress in the Highlands, as the great landlords continued the clearances: driving poor crofters off the land to make way for sheep, which ate less and could be sheared more often. On the death of Donald the Soft in 1799, Alexander MacNabb assumed the ancestral overdraft and a collection of Glen Islet pasture farms. Alexander eschewed the vices that had brought the family fortunes so low and quietly planned the renewal of the MacNabb legacy.

As a young man, Alexander attended one of the first travel seminars held by Thomas Douglas, fifth earl of Selkirk, when he came through Glen Islet to recruit crofters for a settlement along the Thames River in Upper Canada. A few of MacNabb's tenants joined him. Ten years later, Selkirk was back, flushed with success and planning a more ambitious colony in the Canadian west. More of the Glen Islet population went with him.

By this time, the MacNabbs were aristocracy in name only.

* In this task, Ms. Doreen Cameron has been a great help. She arrived at my door one morning soon after our meeting on Hall's Hill and

showed none of the debilitating characteristics of his immediate ancestors. If he was somewhat stern and humourless,
beneath his dour, grey exterior beat the heart of a visionary.

Alexander MacNabb made his first trip to Canada in the
1820s, about the time that his uncle Francis, the twelfth
laird (and the man immortalized by Henry Raeburn on the
Dewar's Scotch label), expired, leaving the family title up
for grabs. It has been in dispute ever since. Some say the
present laird runs a marina on Vancouver Island; others say
he is driving a cab in Albuquerque, New Mexico. Alexander
MacNabb's claim is not mentioned at all in this debate.

The troubles of home must have seemed far away as
Alexander made his way up the St. Lawrence from Montreal,
passing neatly kept farms on the riverbank. In York he was
received cordially by the lieutenant-governor, who treated
him with deference and respect, introducing him as "the
Laird" at elegant dinner parties. MacNabb returned to
Scotland with a vision of building a New Caledonia in the
Canadian bush, with himself as its anointed ruler.

In 1831 MacNabb wrote to the colonial secretary in
London, formally requesting a land grant for his settlers.
The Colonial Office advised him that he would be eligible
for an appointment as administrator of one of the new
townships along the Petunia River. MacNabb could have

---

handed me a volume which is one of the most treasured possessions of
the library. It is a diary written by Fanny Haddock, one of the original
members of MacNabb's party. It begins in the spring of 1832 and pro-
ceeds, with several brief gaps, through to the end of the century. I
cannot believe that such a remarkable document has survived so long
without national recognition. Here is the personal story of a pioneer,
written in her own hand as she carved out a living in the wilderness. Ms.
Cameron also shared with me her own researches on Alexander's
MacNabb's origins.

a free grant of one thousand acres of Crown land and could supervise the settlement of another four thousand acres by his own people at whatever terms he was able to negotiate with them directly. MacNabb agreed. He arrived in York in the fall of 1832 with his wife and three small daughters, along with several cousins and the rest of his followers. They were met at the dock by Captain Charles Fortescue, whose job it was to conduct them into the Persephone wilderness.

Dr. Goulding paints the scene on the morning that the party arrived at the Petunia River to begin the Great Trek west to Persephone.

On the morning of June 14, 1833, MacNabb and his white ox stood in a clearing on the east bank of the Petunia River. Everything about Alexander MacNabb was big. He was a tall man, with a wide face and great whiskers and a prominent nose. His hat was big, his ox was big, and he had a very big opinion of himself. After all, he traced his lineage to the ancient warrior kings of Glen Islet in the turbulent seas of the Middle Minch.

In front of him, navvies swarmed over a great pontoon bridge, securing the last planks in place in preparation for the first crossing of the Petunia River by a party of settlers. On the far bank, the great pine forest loomed like a fortress wall. MacNabb turned and glanced at the members of his party drawn up on the riverbank. Forty-two faces looked up at him in silence, waiting for his command. On the bridge stood Captain Fortescue, in the uniform of the Royal Dragoons. He solemnly drew his sword and pointed it to the west. The bridge was ready.

MacNabb gave a curt nod to a thin-faced man at his side, his kinsman Donald MacKelvey. MacKelvey stuck the reed of his bagpipes in his mouth and blew, filling the woods with the moan of the ceremonial "pibroch."* MacNabb jerked the lead of his ox and stepped up on the bridge. The settlers picked up their belongings, whips cracked, cattle bellowed, waggons creaked, and the Great Trek began.

In that first group of settlers were fourteen families carrying the names MacNabb, MacKelvey, McNab, Cameron, Pargeter, MacKeown, MacEachern, Coutts, Lynch, MacNebb, Haddock, Fisher, Hall, and Bell. Alexander MacNabb was the self-appointed leader of the group and the financier of the seven families who were related to him. These families did call him "the Laird," although it is likely this was due to his forceful personality rather than to any title or special distinction conferred in his homeland. The others in the group referred to him simply as MacNabb.

The MacNabb settlers were a rough agglomeration of Scots crofters, English dock workers, and the graduates of Belfast workhouses. About the only thing they had in common was their religion, which was one brand or other of Protestant. They possessed little more than the clothes on their backs and a few supplies they had puchased in York. Only one couple carried conventional luggage, and they stood out sharply from the rest of the group: Bertram and Fanny Haddock. Bertram was a second son of minor Anglo-Irish gentry who had served without distinction in Wellington's army and was now retired on half-pay. His

---

* The pibroch is a kind of announcement on the bagpipes that cannot be whistled or sung. It goes on until someone offers the piper a drink, usually after about five minutes.

wife, Fanny, was a woman of some breeding, the second daughter of a minister from a parish outside Belfast. Frustrated by a life of genteel poverty and lack of opportunity, they had set out from Belfast to try their luck in the New World and, by a strange set of coincidences, had fallen in with the MacNabb party.*

In her diary, twenty-two-year-old Fanny recorded her impressions of the three-day trip from the bridge through the Demeter Forest towards Persephone: "The thick pine and spruce forest had shaded out all of the undergrowth so that in places no road was necessary to make a passage for the wagons. We passed freely between the trees, many of them three and four axe handles across at the base. The bed of pine needles underfoot was so thick that it muffled the sound of our wagons and oxen. For three days we travelled through the half-light and silence of that great forest."†

At night, the party camped in the open. Each family found a large spruce tree and sheltered under its branches. A fierce thunderstorm broke upon them the second night, but the thick spruce canopy turned the water as efficiently as a shingled roof, and the travellers stayed warm and dry.

On the afternoon of the third day, the MacNabb settlers emerged from the forest and climbed the hill where

---

* The Haddocks' vessel, a rickety timber ship, had sunk off the pier in Portnahaven and left them stranded without passage to Canada. MacNabb's party happened on the pier as the Haddocks were preparing to return home, and he offered the couple a space on board his ship.

† It is a sobering experience to follow that route today, through a vast, mostly treeless plain. Over a distance of twelve miles, there isn't a single one of those great conifers left. Indeed, the only trees within sight of the road are the result of the county reforestation program begun in the 1930s after the topsoil had blown away, the farms had failed, and the land had reverted to the Crown.

Fortescue had enjoyed the view. Looking down into the valley below, they too could see the Pine merging with the meandering course of the Boyne. It being late in the day, they decided to camp on the plateau before going down into the valley.

Fanny Haddock describes the arrival of the settlers the next morning in the meadow that Fortescue had selected as a town site: "We crossed the laughing waters of a stream that tumbles out of the highlands, just at the point where it turns silent and begins its slow march north to the great river and the bay which we had seen the night before from our campsite. We clambered out on the west bank in a lovely glade and put down our burdens in the tall grass. We then watched as the simple peasant folk around us sank to their knees and thanked God for a safe deliverance to this Promised Land."

During his original survey, Fortescue had laid out a town site for the village of Larkspur, a plan consisting of two rows of narrow five-acre lots, divided by a broad main north-south street. The settlers camped within sight of one another on these lots, erecting tents or finding large spruce trees for shelter. MacNabb himself took the lot at the centre next to the river, and his Glen Islet kinsmen – the MacKelveys, McNabs, Camerons, MacKeowns, MacEacherns, and MacNebbs – fanned out on either side. The western lots were taken up by the Irish and the English.

Over the next few days, Fortescue conducted each family to its hundred-acre lot. Most accepted the properties that MacNabb doled out to them on the Pine River plain further downstream from Larkspur. But Bertram and Fanny chose a "property with a nice view and good air movement" a taxing walk from the village on Crown land at the top of Pipesmoke Mountain. It was certainly a pretty place with a commanding view of the Pine River Valley. What the young couple failed to realize was that the change of altitude took them from 5b on the climate and soil map to 4a and reduced their agricultural choices by half.

Fanny seems to have had some misgivings about their selection, noting in her diary that her husband had no knowledge of farming and was somewhat lacking in physical vigour. But she tried to look on the bright side, observing that the property enjoyed a steady breeze and was remarkably free of the bugs that had plagued the party since they had set out from Kempenfeldt.

The settlers spent much of that first summer haggling over property lines and rights-of-way. When the winter winds swept in on September 25, they were still camping under spruce trees. The savage storm that beat down on the valley that day, the first of a series that piled snow knee-deep around them and soon covered the Pine River with a thin layer of ice, finally convinced them to take Fortescue's advice and retreat to the safety of Kempenfeldt. Everyone agreed, except the Halls, Bells, and Pargeters, who felt they were up to the challenge of a winter in the bush. During the six months of the cold, dark winter that followed, something happened to create a misunderstanding between two of the three founding families who remained behind, a rift that has not been healed to this day. From fall to spring, the three families shared a two-room log cabin with nothing but a small mountain of turnips sent out by the government to keep them from starving. Dr. Goulding asserts that sometime in late April 1834, in the middle of yet another snowstorm, "Josiah Pargeter struck Amos Hall with a turnip for no apparent cause, and the families have not been on speaking terms since."*

In May of 1834, MacNabb's party struck out again from Kempenfeldt through the Demeter Forest, rejoined the somewhat haggard Hall, Bell, and Pargeter families, and prepared for the daunting task of clearing the trees from their land grants. But the first priority of the Scots families was to re-establish an institution that had sustained them emotionally and spiritually for so many centuries. With loving and patient hands, they worked together to build a crude brush tent that would house the mysteries of their simple faith. By the end of June, the Larkspur Distillery was complete and producing a respectable two gallons of grain alcohol a week. With a flask in their pockets and a song in their hearts, the settlers marched out to the forest. The sound of axes rang in the Pine River Valley for the rest of the summer.

Speaking of the distillery, Dr. Goulding notes an interesting consequence of the construction of the New Military Road from Kempenfeldt to Larkspur: "Reaching Larkspur under any conditions was a difficult and hazardous journey and could take many days. But building a road made the situation even worse, because as soon as it was finished, thirty-nine taverns sprang up over a distance of thirty-eight miles. Some people with the best of intentions never made it to Larkspur at all. And it wasn't until Prohibition in 1916 that people discovered you could make the trip in an hour and a half."

Every September, the Larkspur Fall Fair opens with the traditional Founders' Parade, a joint project of the

---

* Ms. Cameron advises me that this story was one of the more sensitive items in the Goulding history and may help to explain some of the animosity raised by its publication.

Persephone Township Agricultural Society and other historical and cultural groups. The people who march in the
parade claim to be descended from the first fourteen families of the township.*

Dr. Goulding deflated all such claims by pointing out
that Fortescue had neglected to mention one rather important detail in his survey report. The hard truth was that
none of these families was within a country mile of being
the first to do anything in Persephone. Much of the hinter-
land on the outskirts of settlement in Upper Canada to that
date was already occupied by all manner of escaped con-
victs, runaway slaves, trappers, and wandering bands of
Indians. Persephone Township was no different. It came as
a rude surprise to the pioneers that many of their farms
already had tenants. Rough shanties dotted the landscape,
trails marked the forests, there was a constant coming and
going of people nobody knew. It was certainly not the sort
of empty wilderness they had been led to expect by the
handbills printed up by the Canada Company.

The first families had legal claims to their lots and every
right to enforce them, given the laws of the day, but the
nearest agency that might evict the squatters lay many
days' journey away to the south. In the face of a potentially

* The Halls claim to be the first "arrivals" in Larkspur because on the
evening of June 16 they walked down to the river, where Larkspur now
stands. After scouting the site for a few minutes, they retired back up
the hill to spend the night with the main group. The Bells claim to be
the first "residents" of the township because they were up first on the
morning of the 17th, came down the hill, and got a tent erected on the
site of the present-day fairgrounds. The Pargeters claim to be the first
"farmers" because they chopped down the first tree and began to talk
about a marketing board. Their competing claims raged for nearly a
century before a truce was declared in the 1920s, giving each family a
flag-bearing role in the Founders' Parade.

violent and ugly situation, the MacNabb settlers showed great ingenuity and resourcefulness. They married the squatters into their families as quickly as possible, drove the Indians out, and within a few short months had the place looking just like home. Overnight, the fourteen families became something closer to forty families, who came to dominate the later life of the community.

Even so, forty families would have made only a small impression on a territory as large as Persephone Township. From the moment of her birth, Persephone was marked for speculation. Only a fraction of the surveyed land was taken up for settlement in the first generation. Investors hoping for future profit held the rest. In fact, a glance over the township tax rolls in the early years reads like a gazette of the leading families of the town of York (about to become Toronto). Jarvises, Boultons, Ridouts, and Strachans all held large tracts of the township.

During the first summer of 1834, lots were cleared on the sixth and seventh concessions of the township just south and north of Larkspur. More land was opened to the west of the village up in the highlands in 1835. That year, Fanny's older sister, Adelaide, and her husband, Archibald Smart, came out from Ireland and joined the Haddocks on the lofty heights, providing welcome company in their lonely cabin. By then, Alexander MacNabb had built a lumber mill on his lot on the Pine River in Larkspur and replaced the crude still in the brush tent with a proper stone building. He also built a stone grist mill further up the Boyne River, at a narrows where the present village of Hollyhock is located. All three businesses employed only his own kinsmen.

MacNabb had presented himself to the settlers he had lured across the Atlantic as the owner of the entire grant of five thousand acres, when in fact he was merely the agent for all but ten farms. Any of the MacNabb party could have made their way back to Toronto and applied for a hundred acres of Crown land, but had they done so they would have found themselves on the rocky windswept heights with the Haddocks.

The summer that MacNabb arrived in Persephone, each family was supposed to receive a "location ticket" that described the lot and concession number, its dimensions, and the conditions of settlement. However, MacNabb pocketed the location tickets for the Glen Islet families and instead gave each of them a copy of the piece of paper he had made them sign before leaving Scotland, outlining their duties to him and the sum total of their indebtedness.* These contracts amounted to a combination of mortgage, indenture, and oath of allegiance the like of which hadn't been seen back in the British Isles since the Wars of the Roses, and the fact of which must have been deeply dispiriting to the hopeful newcomers seeking freedom and opportunity. With each passing week, as the Laird MacNabb's

---

* These bonds with MacNabb's Glen Islet kinsmen were contracts in which he promised to provide passage to Canada, food and shelter until they were settled on the land, and, finally, title to a hundred acres. In return, the settler promised to pay MacNabb £35 for every man, £25 for every woman, and £15 for every child under fourteen in his family. In addition, after three years he was to pay one bushel of wheat or Indian corn per acre of land under cultivation "to the Laird and his heirs forever." Free title to the land would be given only if the total debt was repaid within seven years, with 3 percent interest. MacNabb must have known how unlikely that possibility would be in a land where grain prices were in a serious depression and trade with the British Isles had slowed to a trickle. He also reserved to himself the timber rights, hunting and fishing rights, mineral rights, and the right to hunt his horse over the property at any time – as soon as he got a horse.

grip grew tighter, their life in Persephone grew more and more like the one they thought they had left behind.*

MacNabb imposed a strict rule on his kinsmen's contact with the outside world and did his utmost to control the lives of the other families as well. He announced that the settlers needed his permission to travel across the township boundary, and he required everyone to purchase their supplies through him and to sell any surpluses to him at the price he named. For the first two years after the Great Trek, few settlers had any money to spend anyway. In the absence of hard currency, MacNabb carved wooden tokens and set up an exchange system for labour and goods for which he alone set the prices. He paid the settlers for their grain and vegetable crops, then took the tokens back when he supplied them with tools and small luxuries like tea and sugar shipped up from the city. Very soon every settler owed something to MacNabb's general store in Larkspur and its satellite in Hollyhock. Although the "free" families not bound by the Glen Islet contracts were under no obligation to obey him, his monopoly of the store made him a difficult man to cross.

By the close of 1835, with two mills and a distillery humming with business and a virtual monopoly on all trade into and out of Persephone, MacNabb was well established, not only as the financier and political leader of the group but also as the township's first merchant and employer. He erected a toll gate and post office at the Petunia River Bridge to skim the incoming traffic of new settlers. Meanwhile, Fortescue had surveyed Demeter and

---

* These terms were very similar to contracts made by another "Laird," Archibald McNab of Perth, Ontario. See *McNab – The Township*, by Peter Hessel (Kichesippi Books, 1988).

Pluto Townships and was busy conducting and locating new settlers to these places.

By 1836 the Laird and the Captain were a team, expert in manipulating land and settlers to their own advantage. The two began making trips to Toronto to meet immigrants on the wharf, offering them similar terms to those given the Glen Islet families. In this way they delivered at least thirty gullible Scottish and Anglo-Irish families to the area and bound them to a life of servitude in the highlands. They also established a community of French and Irish Catholics on the edge of the forest in Demeter and yet one more colony of Germans, Swedes, and other non-English-speaking nationalities in Pluto Township.

Regardless of their origins, the settlers complained that there always seemed to be money for one of MacNabb's pet projects – the stone to build his general store, an iron-mongery, and grain storage – but when it came to the subject of a church or a school, they were gruffly told to build it themselves.

Amos Hall took the lead in church-building in Larkspur, donating a portion of his five-acre town lot on which he and his neighbours erected a log cabin for the Presbyterians to worship in. He also set up an outdoor school for the children. The hostility between the Halls and the Pargeters flared up again when Josiah Pargeter announced he would be the schoolteacher. Before long, Amos Hall was objecting to Josiah's interpretation of the Scriptures and the schism deepened. Amos withdrew his children from the school in protest and left the First Presbyterian Church. He soon moved out of Larkspur and founded the New Congregational Church and Free School at the base of his hundred-acre farm on the great hill east of Larkspur. This was the local landmark that became known as Heretic's Hill, then True Church Hill, and soon enough just plain Hall's Hill.

Persephone's residents now divided along yet another religious line, with some farmers sending their children into the village to the Presbyterian school and many town residents sending their children out to Hall's Hill to the Free School. As they passed on the road, the children threw rocks at each other and got into fistfights.*

It was only a matter of time before someone would challenge the Laird's rule. That someone was Dougald Cameron, a white-bearded patriarch of the Cameron family. The Camerons had an uneasy relationship with the MacNabbs, having played a leading role in the Glen Islet uprising a generation before. Sparks flared again between the two clans in the spring of 1835, when Cameron rented MacNabb's ox to till his fields and the two men disagreed on the payment terms. MacNabb imposed a punishing rate of interest and forced Cameron into a swap of lands. When Cameron couldn't pay his annual bushel of wheat on the new farm that fall, MacNabb evicted him and his family by force, with the help of the MacKelveys. Cameron took the case to the spring

* The township boundary between Persephone and Demeter became the dividing line between Catholics and Protestants. In Demeter, the English- and French-speaking residents set up communities on either side of the Petunia River. As new settlers arrived, it was just assumed they would stick with their own kind. If, by some awful mix-up in the land office, a French-speaking Catholic family found itself up on the highlands in Protestant territory, the leaders of the community would quickly step in and "relocate" them to a lot on the south side of the Petunia River in Demeter where they belonged. In Pluto Township, where virtually every family spoke a different language and no one could understand anyone else, something like harmony prevailed. The Plutonians were the first people to build a community hockey arena in southern Ontario.

assizes in Kempenfeldt in 1836, but the judge ruled that he had no case because he couldn't prove he owned the land. MacNabb had all the deeds in his possession, and the piece of paper in Cameron's hands was just a lease. Thus Cameron was merely a tenant, and if he couldn't meet the terms of the lease, MacNabb was entitled to throw him out.

The court's judgment stunned the Glen Islet settlers. Finally they understood that their contracts with the Moses who had led them to the Promised Land of Persephone amounted to indentured servitude. The next morning, a crowd of angry settlers met in the New Congregational Church at the base of Hall's Hill. The young Camerons called for a lynching party, but Dougald showed greater restraint. He reminded the young men that laying hands on the Laird would provoke an endless blood feud between the MacNabbs and the Camerons. As the oldest resident in the settlement, a voice respected by all, he was able to persuade his fellow farmers to proceed cautiously. He proposed that they draw up a petition against MacNabb, listing all of their complaints, and send it to the lieutenant-governor. The men agreed, and one of the young Cameron boys carried it off to Kempenfeldt that afternoon on Dougald's ancient horse, Culloden. They took up a collection to pay the toll across the Petunia River.

The answer was not long in coming. It read:

To Those Whom It May Concern:
The Lieutenant-Governor has commanded me to advise you that the arrangements between Alexander MacNabb and his followers are of a purely private nature and of no concern to this Government. He further admonishes the settlers of Persephone to

show obedience to those placed in authority over them and submit to the laws of the land.

J. Joseph,
Secretary to Sir Francis Bond Head,
Lieutenant-Governor of Upper Canada
15 May 1836

And so the pioneers of Persephone went back to their plows and nursed their grievances, awaiting the time when their strength would be sufficient to beard the Laird in his lair.

Among the founding families, the Haddocks and the Smarts seem to have been the least affected by the Laird MacNabb's iron rule. The steepness of the track down into Larkspur and the depth of the winter snows insulated them from the simmering discontents of the village as effectively as if they lived in another country. Both families were blessed with children during the 1830s. Fanny produced twin boys in 1835 and named them Castor and Pollux, after the Gemini twins, who were the Greek gods of the manly arts of wrestling, boxing, barrel racing, and bull riding. Adelaide gave birth to a son, whom she named George Gordon, in honour of the poet Byron. Fanny later produced a girl, Calliope, named after the muse of heroic poetry.

In the late autumn of 1836, Fanny wrote a letter to her aunt back home in Ireland.* From it we get a glimpse of what life was really like for a pioneer family in the Canadas.

* The letter appears in a book I came across in the Larkspur library, a collection of Fanny's correspondence to her Irish relatives assembled by one of her many Canadian admirers, who gathered them during a research trip to Ireland some years ago. The letter quoted here was read on late-night CBC Radio on a program about nineteenth-century life aired in the summer of 1983, as part of the series *The Lost Pioneers of Canada*. The collection was later published, with the aid of a Canada Council grant, by Acid Rain Press.

We are up and doing well before dawn, darning our clothes with needles made from the prickly pear which flourishes everywhere upon the farm and bracing ourselves with a mug of burdock tea. After a full breakfast of a boiled potato and a leaf of salted cabbage, we shovel a path through the snow to the barns where the snorting and coughing of the animals greets us. We fill their mangers with cedar branches and pine cones and turnip peelings and then make our way to the fields, where we spend the morning clawing under the snow looking for stray kernels of grain we might have missed last fall. Archie has a great singing voice and he renders the "Lament of the Kerry Massacre" most admirably and cheers us all. We continue thus until one or more of our party faints from hunger or complains too much of the frostbite. Then it is off back to the cabin for another meal of turnip with a cabbage sauce, or sometimes cabbage with a turnip sauce. Father shot a crow yesterday, which we stuffed and roasted. The twins laughed and clapped as Father and Mother snapped the wishbone between them and made their secret wish together . . .

Nonetheless, the tension in the community around them was nearing the breaking point. As Dr. Goulding observes: "This idyll of frontier life was about to be overturned by a social earthquake that would alter the infant township for good."

This sketch was recently discovered among the effects of Adelaide Smart, on the back of a recipe for roast fool hen. It shows her sister, Fanny Haddock, heroine of the Rebellion of 1837 in Persephone, leading a nanny goat through enemy lines to warn the rebels that their cause was lost.

Chapter 3

AUTOCRATS AND REBELS
1837

———— •◆• ————

My grandfather's account of the part played by the men and women of Persephone in the Upper Canada Rebellion of 1837 has proved to be an antidote to the version I was taught in high school history class. In those days, it struck me that the abortive rising of the common people against the oppressive British colonial powers had failed as both a revolution and a drama. Compared with America's War of Independence, it was pretty limp stuff. Our rebellion lasted but a few days, and our rebels were hardly as memorable as George Washington, Nathan Hale, or Betsy Ross. This is not to say that it wasn't important. On the contrary, it jolted the Colonial Office in Britain into action, and eventually London granted responsible government to the Canadas. The country was placed firmly on the road of peaceful transition to nationhood. But as a story to inspire young students with burning patriotism, it just didn't work.

So I was startled to learn from Dr. Goulding's book that Persephone was the scene of enough "dark intrigue and bloody violence to rival the main events at Montgomery's Tavern in Toronto."

The leader of the Upper Canada rebels was William Lyon Mackenzie, the publisher of the fiercely radical *Colonial Advocate* and later weekly newspapers that regularly exposed the self-dealing of the Family Compact in withering editorials. The historian Thomas Raddall describes the excitable Scot as "a jerking bundle of nerves and vituperation whose feet could not reach the floor when it sat on a common chair, whose great head sat on the diminutive body like an absurd rag doll's, whose eyes glared blue fire in every direction but one – for Mackenzie could never look an opponent in the face."* There's a large portrait of Mackenzie in the entrance hall of the Legislative Building at Queen's Park. He looks about as charismatic as Elmer Fudd. Sir Isaac Brock, the hero of Queenston Heights, occupies the panel across from him, and from his outraged expression it would appear he thinks Mackenzie should have been hung somewhere else a long time ago.

My grandfather's version of the rebellion offers heroism, suspense, violence, and property damage, just the sort of thing to keep teenage boys alert in history class. To steer a steady course through the historical fog, he resorted to what contemporary literary critics call "creative non-fiction." This is the ever-popular technique of filling in the gaps where no known historical evidence exists in order to support a really neat theory or provide a dramatic plot twist. Hollywood scriptwriters have used this approach effectively to show that a murderous bandit like William Wallace was actually a freedom fighter in the cause of Scottish nationalism

---

* Thomas Raddall, *The Path of Destiny* (Doubleday Canada, 1957), p. 379.

(*Braveheart*). Or that the British had to be driven out of America during the revolution because they were burning churches filled with devout Quakers (*The Patriot*).

On my explorations around Persephone, I was struck by the number of "Mackenzie Slept Here" signs on various bed and breakfasts in Larkspur and the highlands. If I were to take these claims at face value and combine them with the claims made by all the other inns and stables in Ontario where Mackenzie is supposed to have bedded down that December, I could only conclude that he suffered from some sort of sleeping disorder.

Did William Lyon Mackenzie come to Persephone? Dr. Goulding claims that he most certainly did. My grandfather's account of the origins of the rebellion provides a useful starting point.

In the dark of the night in March of 1837, a cutter pulled by two horses left the River Road and clattered up the Old Mail Road towards the farm operated by Bertram and Fanny Haddock. The driver was a neighbour to the Haddocks, an Irish drumlin farmer named Terence Lynch. Showing no light, he peered intently into the gloom, shielding his eyes from the sting of ice pellets. His passenger was a tiny bird-like man with a prominent forehead and a shock of unruly red hair, who clutched a satchel with one hand and clung tightly to the dashboard with the other. They drove in silence until the gasping horses reached the summit, where they halted for a few minutes to let the horses catch their wind.

"'Tis a night fit for nair man nair beastie," muttered the driver to his companion whose gaze was fixed on the horizon ahead of him. "Aye," said the little man. "And a pairfect night it is for the business at hand."

A tiny light beamed twice in the darkness ahead of them. The driver started forward. "There!" he whispered. "It is the signal." He uncovered a lamp on the floor of the cutter and held it up once, lowered it, and held it up again. In a few moments they heard footsteps on the road ahead of them and a face appeared at the horses' heads. Fanny Haddock's brother-in-law, Archie Smart, had come out to meet them.

"Major Smart," whispered the driver. "Is the way clear?"

"Ay, neighbour Lynch," said Archie. "And who do we have here?"

"May I present to you Mr. William Lyon Mackenzie."

The lantern shone again and the little man's muffler dropped from his face. He grinned from ear to ear and his eyes gleamed.

"Take me to your people, Major," said Mackenzie. "There are great doings afoot."

Archie Smart led the cutter to the log shanty that dominated the commanding height of the Haddock farm, where Fanny stood guard with another signal lantern. She threw open the door and hustled the men inside. A crowd of expectant farmers from every corner of the Old World stood silently in the little cabin, and their drawn faces revealed the grave risk they were about to take. They were no strangers to risk. They had crossed a dangerous ocean, travelled overland on bone-jarring roads farther than any biblical Israelite, carved out a home in a rough and lonely land, all in the faint but steady hope that they might

better themselves and give their children new opportunity. But since placing themselves in the hands of
the Laird MacNabb and his friends in the corrupt
administration of the province, they had been
deceived, swindled, and reduced to serfdom. Now
they were ready to plot rebellion.*

My initial reaction to this passage was one of forcible
disbelief. Mackenzie did travel around the southern
Ontario countryside delivering inflammatory speeches, but
the idea of him making a four-day journey to the fringe of
settlement in Upper Canada to meet with this motley group
of farmers pushes the limits of credibility. And the sources
Grandfather quotes to back up this story do not add any
weight to his end of the teeter-totter: "Over the years, I
have consulted a number of elderly residents in the drumlins southwest of Larkspur, and at every kitchen table, I
have heard essentially the same version of the rebel chieftain's visit."

Well, good heavens. If I threw in all the stories people
tell in the drumlins and treated them as historical fact, this
book would soon be too heavy to lift. Some people insist
that Louis Riel attended the Petunia Crossing Catholic
School in Demeter Township. Others claim that Darcy
McGee's assassin lived out his days in a remote cabin in the
county forest. There are two ancients at the bar in the
Commercial Hotel who will tell you about a shootout with
Al Capone in the Pluto Marsh. They'll also tell you that
Jesse James visited here in 1881 and buried gold from a

---

* If all the various claims of local histories and oral family traditions are
taken at face value, it would appear that no fewer than three hundred of
Persephone's farmers pressed into the Haddocks' log cabin on that blus-
tery night in 1837. Fanny Haddock places the number closer to seven.

train robbery in somebody's barnyard. Lots of barnyards have been dug up but so far no gold has been found.

I discussed the Mackenzie question with Ms. Cameron while we were leafing through Fanny Haddock's diary, which is the only contemporary local source for the Upper Canada Rebellion and a document Dr. Goulding never saw. Surely, I mused, some small hint of such a meeting must have appeared in these pages if Fanny was the hostess. Ms. Cameron then drew my attention to a recipe for boiled pigeon that had been pasted onto the page dated March 15, 1837. The passage of time had caused the glue to dry out and crumble to dust, and one corner of the recipe had separated slightly from the page. Ms. Cameron donned her dainty archival gloves and gently lifted the corner of the recipe.

"There is writing underneath," she said, peering intently at the yellowed paper.

"Can you read anything?" I asked.

"It says something about 'fat landowners and church-men' . . . 'a fight for self-government and liberty' . . . '"Shall we not be masters in our own house?" said Mr. M. –'"

Ms. Cameron looked at me in amazement. "It's Mackenzie. He was there!"

It took several days to steam the recipe pages off several diary entries for 1837, but the effort yielded a report of the meeting in Fanny's cabin and a description of the preparations the rebels made in the drumlins in the days leading up to Mackenzie's fateful march down Yonge Street in December of that year.

"His talk of a small force moving quickly to seize the city hall in Toronto made me catch my breath," writes Fanny. "Bertram covered his head in a blanket and whispered 'Treason!' But the little fellow jumped off his bench

and said, 'The fat landowners and the churchmen will call
it so, but the world will see it as a fight for self-government
and liberty. Shall we not be masters in our own house?' said
Mr. M. I must confess I was expecting a taller man . . ."

It puzzled me at first why the Smarts and the Haddocks
would support such a dangerous cause as a rebellion against
the British authorities. As former army officers, the husbands should have been enthusiastic supporters of the
Crown. Neither of the sisters showed any political interest
at any stage of the rest of their lives, apart from a vigorous
instinct to root for the underdog. But then, it is possible
that Fanny and Adelaide saw more clearly than most gen-
tlewomen of their day the ruthless exploitation of their
fellow settlers. They could also afford to be less fearful of
MacNabb than the others under his thumb. And, of course,
they were Irish . . . "Mr. M. prepared a commission for
Archie, appointing him an officer of the rebel forces in
Persephone and giving him authority to raise recruits.
When the signal for the rising is given, Archie is to move
with his men to seize MacNabb's bridge."

If there was one symbol that could have united the settlers, it was the hated toll bridge over the Petunia. Even if
a settler was determined to defy the Laird's edict, few could
spare the loose change required to cross that bridge. The
combination of MacNabb's prohibition of trade outside the
settlement and the cost of the toll turned every resident into
a virtual prisoner.

Fanny later reports that her sister's husband, Archie,
threw himself into his work as ordnance officer with great
energy. He arranged to smuggle a quantity of blasting
powder out of the McQuarrie Quarries and hid it in the root
cellar of the Haddocks' log shanty. Bertram watched the
powder being carried to his basement and, in a rare burst of

energy, dropped his axe beside his maple tree and set off to the bush to lay a trapline.* He stayed there for months.

The summer of 1837 was one of the coldest on record in Persephone Township, and killing frosts laid low the crops. The grim settlers braced themselves for war. The Irish drumlin farmers in the highlands had the least to lose and were the most enthusiastic recruits to the rebel cause. They drilled in the bush and practised bayonet manoeuvres with the pitchfork, and their women stitched a banner out of homespun cloth. Meanwhile, down in Larkspur, Captain Fortescue and Alexander MacNabb were organizing a local militia to defend against rebel attacks. MacNabb's mill hands and close kinsmen already constituted a local police force, acting as bailiffs and enforcers for the Laird. Captain Fortescue used this group to form the core of the first formal military unit in the area, the Petunia Valley Foot Regiment. He personally assumed command, promoting himself to the rank of colonel.

The settlers who farmed the fertile Pine River plain downstream from Larkspur were of two minds about the looming conflict. They would have welcomed the downfall of the Family Compact if it meant a chance to oust MacNabb, but they were cautious about open rebellion. When Fortescue called out the Petunia Valley Foot in September, they sullenly appeared on the banks of the Pine River in front of MacNabb's store. Everyone was suffering the effects of the black frosts.† A dangerous quiet hung over the township.

---

* Bertram had been chopping away at a maple tree from time to time since he had arrived at the farm. It had a big notch on one side, but it did not fall over until 1842.

† Black and white frosts still occur to this day. A white frost becomes a black frost when a farmer has no crop insurance, no milk quota, and no position on the township road crew.

By the time Mackenzie gave the signal to his supporters that a date for the uprising had been set, he might as well have placed an ad in the Coming Events section of a late-November edition of the *Constitution*. The news hit Sir Francis Bond Head's desk in Toronto long before it reached the rebels in Persephone. Sir Francis quickly prepared his militia to defend the city. He also sent riders to outposts to warn government representatives to be on the alert for attacks against public institutions.

Dr. Goulding resumes the story.

Early on the morning of December 7, the rebels descended the Old Mail Road and the River Road and set off along the New Military Road on foot towards Kempenfeldt, carrying a banner that bore the Rift rattlesnake in a defiant pose and the slogan "Death to Tyrants." They marched resolutely more than a mile through the forest before stopping to refresh themselves in the Hillhouse Hotel and picking up more recruits. On the 8th they made better time, marching nine miles and passing eight taverns before stopping in the Smithydale Inn. The morning of the 9th found them hidden in the bush a hundred yards from the Petunia River bridge and post office. The tollgate was occupied by an eighty-five-year-old veteran of the American Revolution, James Plunkett. Taking advantage of Plunkett's poor eyesight and stone deafness, the rebels advanced on the building, relieved him of his fowling piece, and tied him to a nearby tree. Then, on the theory that the government's supply lines should be interrupted, Archibald Smart laid one of the barrels of gunpowder from the McQuarrie Quarries under the piers on the west bank. Then he and the company retreated a hundred yards to wait for the explosion.

This was more like it. As a thirteen-year-old, I would have taken a keen interest in historical accounts of mayhem and property damage that occurred on my very own doorstep. As I read my grandfather's words, despite myself I felt a thrill of pride thinking of those wild-eyed freedom fighters from the hills of Persephone, striking at the petty tyranny of the Family Compact. Even if an undefended toll bridge with a post office was their primary target.

Back in Larkspur, Fanny and Adelaide were both worried about the safety of Archie. (Bertram was still out on his trapline in the bush.) Fanny persuaded Adelaide to watch the children as she set off down to Larkspur to investigate. She found the village an armed camp, with the Petunia Valley Foot guarding the New Military Road in the direction of Kempenfeldt. On the pretext of buying some sugar, she slipped into the store, where she saw MacNabb standing on the countertop with Fortescue.

"I have known the plottings of these traitorous curs for months," boasted the Laird. "My young nephew from Kempenfeldt has just brought news as golden as his bonnie head of hair: the rebellion has failed, and Mackenzie's rebels are marching down Yonge Street into a trap. They will all be hanging from the lampposts by nightfall."

Fanny was horrified as she listened to the young man tell the crowd that the militia of Kempenfeldt had been alerted to the gathering of Persephone's rebels at the bridge and was now advancing by forced marches along the New Military Road to cut them off. Fortescue ordered the Petunia Valley Foot to prepare to block the rebels' retreat.

Here is Fanny's unvarnished account of the exploit

that has passed into popular lore as "Fanny's Ride for the Rebels."

I wasted not a moment. I withdrew from MacNabb's store and ran down the street to the home of Flora MacKeown, who knew our cause and wished us success, despite her obligations to MacNabb. Flora lent me a goat, which I fastened around the neck with a cord. Then I set off down the street as fast as I could go without drawing attention to myself. At the New Military Road, I came to a barricade of cedar rails guarded by two slovenly MacNabbs. One of them stepped forward with a musket to block my way.

"And where might you be going, Mrs. Haddock?" he demanded.

I said, "I am conducting this goat to the Cameron farm. She is in season and in need of the services of young Bingo, his billy."

"No one passes this point, by order of the Colonel Fortescue and the Laird MacNabb," said the lout.

"And a brave soldier you are, defending the road against a lady and her goat. Then I will sit down and wait till the order is lifted," I said and made myself comfortable on a stump.

After a long time when I thought I would have to throttle the man, he finally shrugged his shoulders and waved me through.

"Go on with you," he said. "And take that foul-smelling animal too."

I passed through the barricade and, once out of sight of the guards, took to the woods where I ran as fast as my feet would carry me to the farm of Dougald Cameron. Dougald saddled old Culloden for me and I rode hard along the road towards the bridge and the rebel force.

Dr. Goulding picks up the story from here.

Fanny galloped along the New Military Road on her stout workhorse. At each tavern, she reined up long enough to shout, "The rebels are routed!" and galloped on. In the last hour of daylight she reached the Petunia River Bridge, where she found Archie and the rebels locked in furious discussion. They had already lit the fuses for the explosives but were on the wrong side of the bridge to march on Toronto. The sight of Fanny thundering up on a horse lathered white with sweat brought them all running from the bridge to hear her news.

In breathless gasps she told them that the cause was lost, that they must hurry away through the forest to escape MacNabb's trap behind them. Archie bravely made to scramble down the bank to extinguish the fuse on the powder kegs, but strong hands restrained him. The rebels retreated to a safe distance on the Larkspur side of the bridge and waited for the explosion. When the blast came, it separated the bridge from its moorings so that it drifted out in a wide arc downstream. It also set fire to the toll house and post office, which went up in a tower of black smoke.

Just then, the Kempenfeldt militiamen appeared on the roadway across the river in their plain grey uniforms and rough boots of beefhide sewn like moccasins. They approached the riverbank with their muskets levelled.

Fanny wrenched the staff from the hands of the

rebel flagbearer and ripped the rattlesnake from its moorings. She then reached into her bodice and pulled out a substitute banner she had prepared secretly, which bore the words "Persephone's Loyal Volunteers," painted in large letters, and the Union Jack. She tied it to the staff and handed it back. She commanded the rebels to fire into the woods to the west and then advance while cheering loudly. She mounted her horse and plunged into the river.

The Kempenfeldt militia commander was astonished to see this raven-haired woman clutching the mane of the horse, surging through the icy currents of the Petunia, and he ordered his men to hold their fire.

Fanny emerged on the east bank, leapt from her horse, and presented the rebel banner to the commander. She told him the insurgents had blown up the bridge but her "loyalists" had surprised them and captured their standard. She thanked him for his timely appearance, which had caused the scoundrels to scatter. In a few more moments, she claimed, wide-eyed, "Persephone's Loyal Volunteers" could have been wiped out. As the commander accepted the banner, he told Fanny that the rebellion in Toronto had indeed been crushed and Mackenzie and his followers were fleeing for the American border. Worse still, she learned that Mackenzie's satchel had been found in Montgomery's Tavern before it burned, and it contained a list that betrayed the names of every man in the little printer's carefully organized districts between Toronto and Lake Huron. She feared that Archie's name would be in that book.

Promising to "give chase" to the rebels, Fanny remounted her ancient steed and waded back across

the river. She left the militia commander scratching
his head at her story and wondering where to march
his troops. Being a Protestant Scot, he eventually
decided to follow the north bank of the Petunia
downstream to the French Catholic settlement in
Demeter, a certain incubator of rebel sentiment.
Fanny led a forced march of her menfolk through the
forest, around Fortescue's ambush, and up the River
Road and the Old Mail Road to the safety of the
drumlins of Persephone. It is a tribute to her leadership that a journey which had taken three days to
complete in one direction was accomplished in eight
hours on the return. It is probably the longest walk
without a drink taken by the farmers of Persephone
in the nineteenth century.

Once back in the farmhouse, Fanny and Adelaide
told Archie he must flee the country before the lieutenant-governor's men came to arrest him. Hastily
packing some shirts and hardtack into a flour sack,
they pressed their few coins into Archie's hand and
said farewell at the edge of a clearing by the Haddock
farm. Archie Smart set off on foot along a snow-
covered trail, turning to wave once before the forest
folded him from their sight.

After all the excitement my grandfather describes, I
would have expected the authorities to descend on
Persephone with the bayonet and the noose. But for the
longest time nobody came. Colonel Fortescue twice led the
Petunia Valley Foot the length of the New Military Road,
looking for the rebels with no result. When he suggested a
third foray, they lost interest and returned to their families.
But Fortescue could congratulate himself on a brilliant

campaign during which he had lost not a single man to enemy fire. At a moving ceremony on the steps of MacNabb's General Store in Larkspur, the Laird himself awarded Colonel Fortescue a decoration for bravery and hard work. It can be seen on Fortescue's tunic in his campaign photograph many years later: from a silk ribbon imprinted with a beaver rampant hangs a brass lion's head.

Thanks to Fanny's cool head and quick action, a catastrophe had been averted. The postmaster and tollkeeper at the Petunia River Bridge suffered no ill effects, having been tied on the sheltered side of the tree when the powder went off. The rebel troop, the workhorse Culloden, and the heroic nanny goat all went back to their respective farms and waited to see what would happen next.

Four months went by and still no British regulars appeared in Persephone. Finally the rebel farmers decided to risk another secret meeting in the Haddock cabin. Once again, Dougald Cameron suggested a formal petition to the government. This time the farmers agreed. The reply they received was prompt and soothing. Fanny felt confident enough about the situation by that time to write openly about it in her diary.

> April 15, 1838. Great news from the capital! The Colonial Office has dismissed Sir Francis Bond Head, who has been replaced by Sir George Arthur. He writes to us that the Government has not imposed martial law and will take pains to ensure that no citizens shall be subjected to the "unreasonable and arbitrary control of any individual." This has given us a great relief and we dare to hope that we may pass through this time of trouble without violence.

When the long arm of the law finally reached into Persephone that summer, it arrived wearing the red coat and brass buttons of a lone officer of the Toronto Dragoons and the frock coat of a private investigator by the name of Stewart Derbshire. The new governor general of the Canadas, Lord Durham, had dispatched Derbshire on a fact-finding mission to the rural areas in search of the causes of the rebellion. The officer carried a warrant for the arrest of several rebels, but both men seemed more interested in asking questions than in supervising a manhunt. Derbshire chatted with people on the street and in MacNabb's store.

He was, in fact, interviewing some of the petitioning farmers when a rider galloped into town with the news that the Americans had attacked across the border into Canada.* The information had an electrifying effect on the citizens of Persephone, Demeter, and Pluto Townships. They might have had their religious and economic differences with one another, with MacNabb, and with the Family Compact, but an attack by the Americans on Canadian soil was something that instantly brought every resident shoulder to shoulder in a common purpose.†

Once again, the Petunia Valley Foot Regiment formed

---

* Hoping to take advantage of the political crisis in Canada, a rogue band of ruffians called the Hunter Society had launched a raid across Lake Ontario to provoke a war between Britain and the United States.

† The Americans have been taking regular swipes at Canada over the last two centuries or so, and I suppose we should be grateful they no longer shoot at us. They are much more civilized now and just whack us with punitive tariffs and make jokes about us on talk shows. We've sent them back across the border several times with their ears stapled to their hats, which really irritates them because they have had to rewrite all their history books to explain how they really won the War of 1812 and weren't that interested in capturing Quebec in 1776 anyway.

up on the banks of the Pine River in the little meadow beside MacNabb's store in response to the rallying call of MacKelvey's pipes and the church bells. This time there was to be no shirking. Three hundred men from all corners of Pluto, Demeter, and Persephone streamed into Larkspur. It was the sort of spectacle that would have thrilled the young Queen Victoria – she was always delighted by the sight of a variety of nationalities and faiths drawn up in splendid uniforms to defend the Empire.

But these men were in no mood for parade ground displays. They itched for an excuse to fight with someone or something. As my grandfather explains, they got their wish.

Old Dougald Cameron, leaning on the sword his grandfather had dropped at the Battle of Culloden in 1746 and his father had thrown away during the Glen Islet Mutiny in 1788, declared his men's unflinching loyalty to Her Majesty and willingness to serve in the defence of the country. But he demanded that an officer of experience and good judgment be chosen to lead that company – not Fortescue or MacNabb. The men of Persephone, Irish and Scots alike, cheered lustily for Cameron and raised their hats on their pikes and muskets. MacNabb ordered Cameron out of the ranks for discipline, detailing two of the MacKelveys to place him under arrest. Howls of outrage greeted this treatment of the doughty old Scot.

The polyglot soldiers of Pluto, who spoke little English and had trouble following the conversation, shouted that they were not afraid to fight for their young Queen. Dougald Cameron muttered something sarcastic about his dog understanding plain English, which got the Europeans grumbling to one another, asking what he had said. Fritz Bakker, a German from Pluto, boomed: "My hound knows enough to watch the man in the dress who steals the sheep."

Then a voice rang out from Demeter Company. "There's Ulstermen for ye. Right behind ye in the charge, and whoopin' out ahead of ye in the retreat. They're nothin' but cowards."

A voice called back from Persephone Company. "Cowards, did you say, ya slave of Rome? Come over here and say it to my face, you withered daffodil!"

No one knows who fired the first shot. Some say it was a mudball that flew out of Pluto Company and struck Cameron on his bald pate. Others say that a knapsack came out of Demeter Company and caught Bakker on the ear. Whatever the trigger, all the frustrations caused by poor harvests, bad food, ghastly weather, land swindles, corrupt bureaucracy, and arrogant authority boiled over. Politics and ideology were forgotten as each man instinctively reverted to primitive tribal loyalties.

The three companies of the Petunia Valley Foot Regiment were drawn up behind MacNabb's store on a grassy slope that led down to the Pine River, some two hundred feet away. A heavy rain the night before had turned the field to sticky mud. Persephone Company commanded the high ground, near the store veranda, while the two other companies stood partway down the hill, Pluto on the right and Demeter on the left. When the battle opened, Persephone found itself threatened from both sides and instinctively divided its forces to take on the two rival townships. The Glen Islet Scots of the Pine River wheeled right to face the "foreigners" from Pluto. The Protestant Irish and English drumlin farmers wheeled left and struck at the Catholic French and Irish from Demeter, who for once held fast together. Although outnumbered two to one, the Persephonites fought stoutly, retreating slowly back up the hill to the veranda of MacNabb's store.

Fingers gouged into eye sockets, teeth bit into ears, boots thunked into shins. The air was filled with the shrieks and groans of the injured. MacNabb and Fortescue were powerless to stop their men. The Laird ordered his piper MacKelvey to sound the Glen Islet Mutiny pibroch, a primal scream that normally brought the men to their senses. It had no effect on the flailing melee, and Fortescue executed an expert strategic retreat across the river to the safety of the bush, not failing to leave his sword on the battlefield, as was his custom.

On the veranda, Dougald Cameron stuck his claymore into the plank floor and shouted, "Here will I stand, and let no man of Glen Islet retreat a step from this place." His sons and nephews stood shoulder to shoulder with their patriarch, dealing terrific blows to any man who approached them. Under a sudden rush by the combined Catholics of Demeter, Persephone's drumlin farmers backed up the muddy slope to the veranda of the store to join the Camerons, but Major Archibald Smart had trained Persephone Company's artillery section well. Even without their leader, they knew what to do.

They dodged around the store's side entrance to a set of back stairs and gained the upper floor of the store, where they slammed the trap door shut and hauled a set of weigh scales over it. Then they opened the windows of the second storey looking out over the battle. Sensing an opportunity in which artillery could prove decisive, they began hurling the previous fall's produce down on the attacking forces: spongy turnips, mouldy apples, and blighted potatoes. Demeter Company fell back in confusion. Screams and yells and the wail of MacKelvey's bagpipes filled the air.

Alexander MacNabb waded through the mud to the edge of the veranda, grabbed Cameron by the shoulders, and shouted that if they did not all leave his store this instant, he would have them shot.

"Load canister!" shouted a voice from the upstairs window. Everybody looked up to see a large butternut squash flying through the air like a football. It caught MacNabb on the forehead and down he went, like a Persephone pine struck with the woodsman's axe. He sank back into his faithful piper's arms unconscious.

Within a few minutes, the men of Demeter lay crumpled in the mud, and their attack collapsed. The drumlin farmers on the second floor returned to aid their brothers of the Pine River, who were now locked in fierce struggle with the men of Pluto in the main room of the store. They whipped open the trap door and fell upon the Plutonians from above with a Gaelic curse. An answering roar came from the Cameron family on the other side of the room. The men of Pluto, realizing they were trapped, cornered, and surrounded, defended themselves with "frying pans, boards, brooms, kettles, and any article that would withstand swift contact with a man's head."

The battle raged back and forth across the room until not a stick of furniture stood unbroken. After several hours the men were obliged to call a short pause while they lit lamps so they could see one another.

MacNabb, meanwhile, had been carried into the store and laid out on the counter. Someone removed the larder keys from his pockets. There the warriors discovered several cooked hams, a cheese drum, and a barrel of rare Glen Islet single malt that MacNabb had been saving. The men still standing on both sides staggered to the bar and ate ravenously for a time, watching the older Cameron brother exchange blows with Fritz Bakker. One by one, the Demeter men revived and stumbled into the store to seek refreshment.

Some nasty wounds were received and exchanged, and the old hero Dougald Cameron was hit so hard on the ear that he died ten years later still complaining of the hurt. By morning, the ham and the cheese and the whisky were gone, and everybody felt much better. MacNabb did not regain consciousness until ten o'clock, when the store was empty and the farmers had all gone home.

Derbshire and his officer watched the entire proceedings from the safety of the upstairs window in the MacKeown house, which still stands on Mill Street in Larkspur. He continued to make notes in his black book and left the next day with a suggestion to the officer that a judicial inquiry be launched into MacNabb's land dealings. He later reported to his employer in Montreal that in Persephone he had found "several nations warring in the bosom of a single township." Durham read this and is reported to have said, "Very good line. I can use that somewhere."

Before leaving this story of the Rebellion of 1837 and its aftermath in Persephone Township, it may be useful to lay to rest a few persistent myths surrounding the events I've just described. For example, one pamphlet recounting Persephone's role in the rebellion claims that four hundred rebels marched on Toronto from the township. Given that the entire population was only 397 in 1841, this estimate seems high.

I can also confirm that the chestnut tree in front of the Larkspur Orange Lodge was not used to hang rebels. The lodge records state that the tree was planted at Confederation in 1867, and a photo from 1875 shows it had grown about eight feet high. I have also heard it said that British troops burned a swath thirty miles wide across the township while searching for rebels. Yet the entire farm population at that time was located within a two-mile radius of Larkspur.

In the end, very few shots were fired, almost all of them at the Battle of MacNabb's Store, and although many found their mark, none was fatal. The story wasn't that much different across the province, where the impact of the rebellion was measured mostly in property damage. Sir Francis Bond Head had ordered the rebel headquarters at Montgomery's Tavern burned to the ground. The site subsequently became a post office. The Petunia River post office, which had been burned by Persephone's rebels, subsequently became a tavern.

Persephone's Loyal Volunteers metamorphosed into a volunteer firefighting brigade that rushes to the scene of grassfires in the drumlins to this day. The Petunia Valley Foot Regiment eventually fielded a very strong brass band that would entertain the community for the next century and a half. Fanny Haddock's makeshift banner now hangs in a glass case in the Regalia Room of the Larkspur Orange Lodge.* The firefighters' motto is "Sic Erunt Novissimi

---

* Sadly, the rebel banner "captured" by the Kempenfeldt militia has been lost.

Primi" – "The Last Shall Go First" (unless you're a local, in which case it translates as "Last In – First Out.")

And William Lyon Mackenzie? I think he very probably did come to Persephone. And I think I understand why he never came back.

If you visit the Hollyhock Mill today, you may spot the old millstone, which lies broken in midstream below the dam. Picnickers who enjoy the mill's picturesque setting, here photographed before its recent restoration and opening as a restaurant, have no idea of the dark events that have haunted the site since a stormy summer night in 1846.

Chapter 4

THE LEGEND OF HECTOR AND ISABELLA

1838 TO 1850

D r. Goulding seems to have been a tireless observer of the war between the sexes in Persephone Township and the forces that brought them together and flung them apart. He makes the observation that "so many bachelors and spinsters looked after invalid mothers into old age that it was surprising the township managed to repopulate itself." But it has. And after a good deal of basic research in the bar of the Commercial Hotel, I think I have a fairly good take on the mating rituals of Persephone Township.

The abduction of Persephone by Hades provided the inspiration for many of the stable marriages in the township over several generations of settlement. Very often, a young man would carry off a girl with the assistance of a few friends and hold her in a cabin in the hills until her reputation was compromised and a deal could be made with her father. Then a dowry of linens, cookware, and livestock would be handed over and the wedding would be celebrated in a local church. Several weeks after the wedding, the community descended on the young couple after midnight in what was called a "shivaree." People would beat pans, fire off shotguns, and play all sorts of elaborate practical jokes, such as putting a wagon on top of the barn or letting all the pigs out into the corn. Heavy drinking and fist fights completed the merrymaking, which often lasted until dawn. Then everyone tottered home to do morning chores.

Sometime later, the bride's father would pick up his son-in-law and take him to a farm sale or for a day's ice fishing or deer hunting, depending on the season. These rambles usually lasted up to a week and would take in all thirty-nine of the taverns along the New Military Road. On their return, father and son-in-law were beaten soundly with brooms and returned to their field work, having forged an emotional bond that often outlasted the marriage. Thereafter the newlyweds might be seen together at a dance or a church picnic, but the husband would always prefer the opportunity to go "down country" with his father-in-law and other male relatives to see about a dog or a firearm. Since the company of women was believed to be a corrupting influence, men developed elaborate rituals to maintain these emotional bonds. Some of these rituals survive today in the form of the shop party, the crop tour, the Pluto Sales Barn Spring Horse Sale, and the Kinsmen Snow Bunnies Poker Run.

By the 1920s, most wildlife had been driven from the township and men were hunting the white-footed meadow vole and the barn swallow to the point of extinction. Fortunately, the invention of the pickup truck transformed rural life and relieved a great burden on the local ecosystem. The pickup gave the men much greater range for hunting and a greater carrying capacity for weapons and beer. The box of the truck also provided armpit support during long and detailed discussions about politics and the mysteries of the internal combustion engine. During dances at the Orange Lodge or on Fall Fair day, the truck provided a refuge from the women. It was normally equipped with "twenty-four on the floor," a supply of stubby Coke bottles that could be used to camouflage the Larkspur rye whisky that was carried in the glove compartment, which was also known as "the bar in the car." Behind the seat there were usually more tools, emergency rations, and smutty reading material than you would find on an oil rig in the Beaufort Sea.

The pickup truck gave a measure of independence and privacy to young couples and considerably reduced the need to abduct women by force, which one can only assume came as a welcome relief for the women. Ministers warned against the evils of this form of transportation from the pulpit, predicting that it would lead to the breakdown of society, but they were largely ignored. Today a young man's search for a girl begins with the purchase of a weather-beaten Ford or Dodge, and he is probably completely unaware that his purchase is the direct result of a steady evolution from primitive Celtic traditions that date from the early part of the nineteenth century.

But back to my story.

I was forbidden to play in only one place on the Boyne River, and that was the millrace at Hollyhock. It was actually my grandmother who issued the edict, and I always thought there was something more to this restriction than the risk that I would lose my footing in the rushing white water. Although my grandmother had married a scientific man, she was a local girl and she owned her own set of local superstitions. Her warning about the Hollyhock Mill derived more from the category of never putting new shoes on the table or not passing someone on the stairs or spilling salt than it did from the rules of Elmer the Safety Elephant.

The stark stone walls of the abandoned mill and the collapsed foundations of the mill house gave the place something of the aura of a ruined Norman castle. If I were a house-hunting ghost in Persephone, the Hollyhock Mill would be a desirable address.

Except that a ghost of long standing already occupies the place. According to a hoary legend, the site is associated with violent death due to supernatural causes. I learned the details in the course of writing this book, and in the process, I uncovered a touching love story that has never been told in modern times.

By the time Alexander MacNabb recovered consciousness following the Battle of MacNabb's Store, his psychological hold on the families of Persephone had been broken. Within little more than a decade, the Larkspur store, mills, and distillery would be in the hands of the MacKelvey family, staunch supporters of MacNabb since leaving Scotland, who acted as his bookkeepers, bill collectors, enforcers, and bailiffs. The MacKelveys were famous for their parsimony and sharp dealing, a trait that made them useful to MacNabb and that has been carried down through the family to the present day. You cannot offend the MacKelveys of Larkspur merely by calling them cheap. They are proud of their reputation and tell stories at their own expense to feed the mystique.*

---

* Dry Cry MacKelvey, who will be familiar to readers of Walt Wingfield's column in the Larkspur *Free Press & Economist*, is the present owner of the MacKelvey stores and feedmill in Larkspur. He once sold a man a wheelbarrow and forgot to make a note of it. When he couldn't remember who the man was, he thought of five people that it could have been and sent out invoices to each one. He got paid four times for the wheelbarrow. (This is a story he tells about himself.)

It is quite odd, considering the strong influence MacNabb had on the founding and early years of the township, that he fades so quickly from the pages of Dr. Goulding's history. My grandfather writes of his wife and family but does not tell us what became of them: "Like a hound with his tail between his legs, MacNabb retreated from Larkspur and molested the residents of Persephone no further. The grand design of a new Glen Islet on the Pine came to naught." In a separate chapter, Dr. Goulding reports that the Hollyhock Mill burned in the 1840s, but he makes no reference to MacNabb's death or final resting place. There is a plaque commemorating him at the Larkspur Town Hall, and someone even went to the trouble of painting a mural in the foyer of the Port Petunia High School immortalizing the Great Trek. But no one seemed to know where MacNabb was buried or whether he even had any descendants. I could find no marker in the Larkspur cemetery for him or his wife.

The reader may be wondering why I do not draw here on local newspaper reports of the period. There certainly were newspapers in Larkspur by 1842. New immigrants streamed into Persephone during this decade and the village's population soared. We know that by 1850, no fewer than six Larkspur newspapers were publishing a weekly edition, including the *Free Press* and its fierce competitor, the *Economist*. In those days, it was a simple matter to buy a small press and run off a single broadsheet, printed on both sides with news and advertisements. These publications should have provided a dependable source of doubtful information. But very few issues of any of these journals survived the remarkably frequent fires that hit newspaper offices during this period, and none that did shed any light on what happened to the Miller MacNabb. It is not until 1855, when the *Free Press* merged with the *Economist* and burned out the last of its remaining rivals, that we find intact newspaper files for any given year.

In search of clues to Alexander MacNabb's fate I therefore resorted to some amateur archaeology. I decided it was time for me to pay a visit to the old mill property at Hollyhock.

On an unseasonably cool early summer day with a stiff wind whistling up the valley and the maple trees releasing their seed pods into the clear and cold waters of the Boyne River, I bicycled up the River Road to Hollyhock. The village itself is a small cluster of buildings at the base of two drumlins where the river narrows to form a rapids. Stone buttresses stand on each bank, all that remains of the old dam. The water has tumbled by them unchecked for longer than anyone can remember.

A stone's throw from the mill site, I found a well-kept pioneer cemetery with about fifty marked gravesites. I strolled among the pocked and pitted headstones, pausing at numerous MacNabbs, McNabs, Camerons, MacKelveys, and Pargeters, but not one paid homage to the life of the Laird MacNabb. As I turned to leave, I nearly tripped over a small man with a wisp of white hair and a pipe clenched in his teeth, leaning on a rake.

"Lookin' for somebody?" he asked. When I explained he said, "There's no Laird MacNabb here. But I got one for the Miller MacNabb." He led me over to the shed that houses the lawn mower. Propped up against the fence by the shed was a white tablet in the shape of a wheat sheaf, much worn but still bearing a faint inscription.

This stone erected to
Alexander MacNabb
Miller of Hollyhock
1781-1846
Drowned in the millpond
By a few of his friends

Here was a puzzle. The name, the year of birth, and the location would identify it as belonging to the legendary laird, but there was no reference to his status as chief of the clan or founder of the settlement, something he would certainly have specified in his will. And the date of death, nine years after the rebellion, fit the circumstantial evidence. Surely, I thought, this shabby little stone couldn't possibly mark the final resting place of such an important figure. It must be a cousin. But then I remembered the memorials to so many other great Canadians: John A. Macdonald's gravesite in Kingston was neglected for years; General Brock isn't even buried under his great tower at Queenston Heights. His remains were eventually moved to a quiet little cemetery in Hamilton. Many others have been allowed to moulder and disappear. I looked more closely at the inscription. Was it only me, or did the words carry the faint whiff of conspiracy? MacNabb had certainly made more than a few enemies, and it would not have been surprising if a group of them had taken the law into their own hands. But surely there would have been an inquiry, a newspaper story, or at least a church record.

"I wouldn't be touching it, if I was you," said the little man.

"I'll be careful," I assured him.

"Not worried about you breakin' anything. Just warnin' you. The curse, you know. Lot of people has came to a bad end around here."

He straightened up and limped off with his rake. I smiled to myself. The Curse of the Hollyhock Mill is a legend that survives only in the oral tradition of the residents of the Boyne and Upper Pine River Valleys. There is no mention of it in Dr. Goulding's history but I suspect that, like the biblical story of the Flood, it may have some historical basis in fact. There are enough renditions of it to confound the cleverest historian, variously featuring patricide, fratricide, a headless horseman, a ghost on the ramparts, and a body under the floorboards. The common thread is that the owner of the Hollyhock Mill died a violent death sometime in the nineteenth century, leaving a curse on the mill property and any who dared disturb it.

Back at the Commercial Hotel, I took up my customary position at the end of the bar and was promptly invited to join a euchre game convened by Amos, Alex, and Andy Fisher, three grizzled cattle farmers who pasture their herds on separate drumlins south of Larkspur. On impulse, I asked them if they could tell me what happened to the Laird MacNabb, and I received three different replies almost in the same breath.

"Struck by lightning," said Amos.

"Drownded," said Alex.

"Burned out!" said Andy.

This is how the oral tradition works. It develops a story in three different directions, adding dialogue and fresh detail as it goes. It's enough to leave the dedicated writer of local history at a loss for words.

Early the next morning, well before half past nine, I was startled from a sound sleep by the ringing of the telephone. It was Ms. Cameron, whose tenacious research efforts had already shed considerable light on some of the more shadowy corners of Persephone's past. She was calling from the library.

"I've been to the Land Registry Office to check on the Hollyhock Mill, as you asked," she said. "It passed out of the MacNabb family in 1850 and was transferred to his nephew, 'Big Sandy' MacKelvey. The MacKelveys have owned it ever since."

"Aha," I said. "That must be the golden-haired nephew who brought the news from Kempenfeldt that the rebellion had failed. Say, do you know the story about the curse?"

Ms. Cameron has an infectious laugh, a musical sound with a pleasant hiccup in it. "Of course," she said. "When I was a little girl, we knew the mill was haunted, and we were all warned never to go near it. But I always thought it was just to keep kids from playing around the old stone walls."

"I wonder," I replied. "Do we know for certain that the Miller MacNabb was the same person as the Laird?"

"Well now, I'm not positive about that. There's somebody you should probably talk to. She's in the Sundown Nursing Home now, but she lived all her life in Hollyhock. She was a good friend of my grandmother's. I'll take you to meet her if you like."

We found Miss Rita MacKelvey listening to the radio in a corner of the nursing home recreation room, where the residents play shuffleboard and do their crafts. She seemed remarkably spry for 104 years old and told us that she amuses herself by collecting bits of string. When I asked her if she knew anything about the last of the MacNabbs at the Hollyhock Mill, her eyes brightened and she gripped my hand.

"A terrible hard man," she said.

"Alexander MacNabb?" She nodded vigorously and I pressed on. "Do you mean the Laird or the Miller?"

"People called MacNabb all sorts of things," she said. "He was Black MacNabb or MacNabb of the Glen. But mostly he was just the Miller MacNabb or MacNabb the son of a –"

"He thought of himself as the chief of the MacNabb clan from Glen Islet, didn't he?" asked Ms. Cameron.

Miss MacKelvey waved a veined hand dismissively. "Pshaw! The MacNabbs was thick as flies on the back end of a sheep in those days. And they all claimed to be descended from Scottish kings. If there ever was a title to the MacNabbs, it wasn't worth a rain in May in Persephone Township. They were all eatin' oatmeal and the odd rabbit like everybody else. But I can tell you what happened to the Miller MacNabb, because my great-grandmother was a girl when the mill house burned, and she told me the story herself."

Miss MacKelvey then related the version of the Curse of the Hollyhock Mill that I have recorded here. The only hesitation I have in accepting it at face value is that she also occasionally claims to be Florence Nightingale and talks incessantly to an invisible dog that the nurses tell me was run over in 1936. Otherwise she makes perfect sense.

"The Miller MacNabb lived with his missus and the wee ones in the stone house beside the mill, and he ground wheat into flour for all the farmers on the Boyne River. These were the years of the terrible black frosts that came in every summer month, killing the wheat crops and crushing the hopes of many a poor family. Whenever a farm failed, MacNabb was there to snap it up, just like a duck on a June bug, so he was.

"He had three daughters, the oldest turnin' sixteen the year of the fire. They were lovely wee things and all the young men of the township were tomcattin' around the mill. But MacNabb was a jealous hard man, like I say, and when he caught the oldest girl in the carriage house of the Hollyhock church with a Cameron boy, he threw a fit that would have put a gander out of the garden, so it would. The Camerons was a good family and always has been." At this point she nodded to Ms. Cameron and smiled. "Just the usual bit of hellery after school's out, but they had never done him no harm. In fact, the very opposite was true, for it was MacNabb that stole Dougald Cameron's farm in the first years of settlement. So they say, anyway.

"So the Miller dragged the girl back to the house and told the three of them they were not to leave his roof except in his company. He had a stonemason brick up the windows of their bedroom and he put iron bars on all the windows on the main floor. The front door had a lock that opened with a single brass key, which he carried on a string around his neck. On Sunday mornings, his three daughters and his wife followed him single file down to the little church in the village for services, and they went home right after without speaking to a soul.

"The girls put up with this for a few months before turning to their mother. But she was a poor timid creature who wouldn't shoo a fly off her own nose for fear of giving offence. Her only advice to them was to ask God for guidance. Well, you know, in a manner of speaking, they did just that. And they got a system going to talk to the Cameron boys by leaving notes in their hymn books at the church. Before long, they had a plan hatched to escape from the mill and row downriver to the bay, where they would hail one of the little freight boats that plied the coastal waters and make their way to the United States.

"MacNabb knew nothing of this plot until a stormy summer night when it was all set to take place. The Cameron boys brought a rowboat up the Boyne River and hid it in the bushes on the riverbank under the girls' window. They knew MacNabb was horrible superstitious about the *caoineag* –"

"The what?" I asked.

"It's a Scottish form of the banshee," whispered Ms. Cameron. "You know, the fairy."

"Yes," said Miss MacKelvey, gripping my hand again and pinning me to the wall with her piercing gaze. "The *caoineag* is the woman fairy that sits below the waterfall and wails before a death. When women keen at a funeral, it is an imitation of her cry. When more than one appears and they wail and sing in chorus, it is for the death of some holy or great person. Sometimes this banshee comes in a black coach in the shape of a coffin drawn by headless horses. It comes rumbling to your doorstep, and if you open the coach, the *caoineag* throws a basin of blood in your face."

"Yikes," I said.

"Miller MacNabb opened the door of his house and one of the Cameron boys splattered the blood of a fresh chicken in his face. That pretty much disorganized his thinking. He fell down in a dead faint. The boys took the brass key from around his neck, freed the girls from the house, and led them down the bank to the rowboat. As they were pulling away from the riverbank, Mrs. MacNabb came out and found her husband lying on the ground, his shirt soaked in red. At this sight she yowled like two cats with their tails tied and slung over a clothesline. It woke up everyone in the village, and they rushed out into the road in their nightclothes.

"Was your great-grandmother there herself to see this?" I asked.

Miss MacKelvey gave me a sharp look. "No, she lived in Larkspur at the time . . . but she remembered it just the same." For a moment I thought I had touched a nerve. Then she took a deep rasping breath and shrieked in a voice that made me and Ms. Cameron jump and caused the patient in the next bed to reach for her oxygen mask.

"'Dinna leave me, my pretty chickens!' screamed Mrs. MacNabb. The sound of her voice brought MacNabb back to his senses. He sat up and felt for his key, but it was gone. As he ran out to the millrace, a flash of lightning showed the boat drifting down the river with his three daughters and the Cameron boys. MacNabb shouted a curse into the howling wind and started pulling boards out of the dam."

"The curse!" I whispered. "Do you remember the curse?"

Her eyes narrowed. "It was terrible. He said, 'You have all inherited a nature so sinful that there is no hope for you. May you live and die under the wrath of a vengeful God and eat the dust of the fields, for though you till the earth, she will not yield up to you her strength. God will forgive only a handful of his Elect on the Day of Judgment, and you shall not be among them.'*

"The water went over the dam in a great rush, washing one stone after another from the foundation until the whole west corner of the mill toppled over into the river and collapsed, taking MacNabb with it. The last thing to fall was the millstone, and it squashed MacNabb flatter than a nit. Then lightning struck the house and it burst into flame. By

---

* This may be seen as overkill, considering what the pioneers had already been through. But it helps explain why none of the houses in the Upper Pine River Valley have had a coat of paint since they were built.

morning, the house was naught but a pile of rubble, and the mill was an empty stone shell."

Miss MacKelvey paused in her story, visibly tired from the effort of remembering. "Did they ever find the girls?" asked Ms. Cameron.

"They searched the river for weeks, but no trace was ever found of the MacNabb girls or the Cameron boys. Some days later, six workers from the mill waded into the river and tried to raise the millstone. It had been brought by steamship and wagon all the way from the Cape Breton quarries and was worth good money. But when the men went to lift the stone, they felt a tremor pass through it that filled their hearts with terror. They dropped the stone and scampered out of the river, but the damage was done. Every single one who put a hand on that millstone died within the year. Ever since then, it has lain in the Pine River and no one has dared to touch it, for fear of the curse of the Miller MacNabb. Well they should, for I believe his bones lie beneath that stone."

Miss MacKelvey closed her eyes and I presumed the interview was over. Yet neither Ms. Cameron nor I made a move to leave. This amazing old woman had just provided the most complete telling of the legend I had yet heard. It had everything, including lightning, fire, and a drowning, just as the Fisher brothers had claimed. I wanted to tell her that there was a modern footnote to her story, which she probably wasn't aware of. The millstone had been moved just recently by Walt Wingfield, who had decided that the curse was all nonsense. He tried to drag it out of the river with a team of horses. No sooner had Walt snagged onto it with the chain than the horses went wild with terror. They dragged it up the bank until it lodged between two trees, nearly killing Walt in the process. A few days later the

stone tumbled back into the river to its former resting place
and broke into three pieces. So it remains.*

The modern historian would be forgiven for throwing
up his hands in despair at the complete absence of any cor-
roborating authority to support the tale that Miss
MacKelvey told. If there were church records for this
period, they must have been destroyed in one of the many
calamitous fires that have wiped out many of the written
records of the township over the last century. The township
files are silent on the subject of a mill catastrophe, and the
Land Registry Office notes only that the mill property was
transferred to the MacKelvey name four years later, a delay
that could be explained by legal proceedings when no
direct heir was present.

And yet, Miss MacKelvey's story has the ring of truth.
For one thing, it dovetails nicely with a recently discovered
piece of physical evidence from that fateful night in 1846.
During the brief interval before the millstone fell back to its
resting place, Walt Wingfield returned to the riverbank,
where he noticed something odd on the river bottom where
the stone had lain. He waded in and reached down to

---

* Some say that the breaking of the stone has lifted the Curse of the
Hollyhock Mill, but others have their doubts. Last summer, a consortium of dentists and tax lawyers restored the building and converted it
to the Laughing Waters Steak House and Pasta Bar. Numerous construction delays plagued the project, and there was constant interfer-
ence from the World Biosphere Protection Agency and the Pine River
Conservation Authority. Several expensive tools and a lot of building
material mysteriously disappeared from the site, although this often
happens when a significant amount of money is being spent on a place
with good road access. Then, just a week after the restaurant opened, on
a moonless night at the stroke of twelve (which was supposed to be the
exact moment that MacNabb was washed over the dam), the chef quit.
The locals nodded to one another knowingly, made the sign of the evil
eye, and muttered darkly that it was tempting fate to charge such prices.

investigate, and his hand closed over a heavy brass door key. That key now rests in a glass case above the fireplace in the main dining room of the mill restaurant, along with a fanciful portrait of the Miller MacNabb holding a dirk in one hand and carrying a sack of grain on his back. A brief treatment of the legend is carried on the restaurant placemats.

However, even if the story was true, it still didn't answer the original question: Was the Miller MacNabb the same person as the Laird MacNabb?

As if in answer to this unspoken question, Miss MacKelvey's eyes snapped open and she said quite distinctly: "It's all in the trunk. You're welcome to look in there and see what you can find. I can't remember any more."

"Trunk?" I asked.

"Yes," she said firmly. "You look in there."

Her eyes closed again. We rose quietly, thanked the nurse at the reception desk, and stepped out into the sunshine.

Before we parted, Ms. Cameron promised to look into the matter of the trunk. She was as good as her word. It seemed that Miss MacKelvey had sold her Hollyhock house ten years before, but none of her relatives knew anything about a trunk. However, a few weeks later Ms. Cameron ran into the new owner of the house, a Toronto dentist, and raised the subject with him. He mentioned that he was just then carrying out an extensive renovation, and the contractor had pointed out a small square hole that appeared to give access to a crawl space above the second floor. He invited us to drive out and take a look in there.

The next morning, Ms. Cameron and I met the new owner at the old MacKelvey place, a rambling two-storey brick farmhouse with a peeling front veranda and a sagging woodshed attached to the kitchen. We found a stepladder, climbed the creaking wooden stairs to the second-floor hallway, and placed it under the access hole in the ceiling. I am not good with tools and Ms. Cameron was wearing a pretty summer frock that stopped just above the knee, so the good dentist offered to ascend the ladder and pry open the hatch with a crowbar. It yielded to his efforts and he was able to force his head and shoulders far enough up through the opening to shine a light around.

"What do you see?" I asked him.

"Oh . . . wonderful things," he replied in a hushed voice.

He squeezed through the hole, and I stepped onto the ladder and peered up over the rafters. It took us a moment to absorb the scene before us. There was an enormous pile of brown glass bottles, each in the distinctive shape of the Larkspur Distillery, and another separate pile of Dr. Thomas's Nerve Tonic bottles. The two collections paid mute testimony to a long and dogged marriage in Miss MacKelvey's family. There were apple crates filled with magazines, books, and children's toys. And over by the chimney, under about six inches of raccoon poop and countless generations of dead cluster flies, stood a steamer trunk of the type popular in late Victorian times. The dentist and I manhandled the trunk out through the opening, got it down on the floor, and pried it open.

"My goodness," said Ms. Cameron. "I don't think anyone has opened this for a hundred years."

As we eased the lid back on the trunk, a shaft of morning sunshine fell on a carefully organized collection of letters, photographs, financial records, newspaper clippings, a family Bible, a wedding dress, and several pairs of shoes, along with countless other keepsakes that spoke of a life richly lived and memories carefully preserved. They were all tagged, dated, and catalogued in a small but legible hand worthy of a museum curator.

For the rest of the morning, time stood still as we carefully picked through the contents of the trunk. By the time we had completed this initial inventory, we realized that we were looking at the most complete collection of one family's history ever to be discovered in this community. And the crown jewel of this precious treasure was a small sheaf of letters tied together with a ribbon. A glance at the first few letters strongly suggested an illicit correspondence between the owner of the trunk and her lover. This discovery took me back to the day I unearthed the sole surviving copy of my grandfather's history.

Several original voices speak to us from Persephone's past: Colonel Fortescue through his scrapbooks, Fanny Haddock through her diaries and her correspondence with Adelaide, a scattering of issues of the *Free Press* and *Economist* newspapers. But much of the unpublished material is self-conscious and seems to have been written with posterity in mind. Here in this trunk were the unvarnished and unedited conversations of two Persephonites from another world. I quickly got on the phone to Miss MacKelvey's great-nephew to ask for instructions on how to handle this archival motherlode.

"Don't lug that trash over here," he said impatiently. "I spent enough of my life emptying out that house."

He heartily concurred with the new owner's suggestion that we place the contents of the trunk in the hands of the Larkspur library, in whose archive room Ms. Cameron and I resumed our inspection of the trunk's contents the following morning.

We soon determined that the trunk belonged to Miss

MacKelvey's great-grandmother, Isabella Pargeter MacKelvey, daughter of Josiah and Euphemia Pargeter, two Great Trekkers who toughed out the first winter in Larkspur in a cabin with the Halls and the Bells. Isabella claimed to be the first white woman born west of the Petunia River (which seems to have been an important distinction to her because she mentioned it quite frequently). There was a photograph of her dating from the 1880s, when she must have been in her early fifties, standing against a studio backdrop of foliage and Ionic pillars. The photo shows a tall, dignified woman with the prominent Pargeter nose that still distinguishes the family and the fierce dark eyes of a bird of prey. A formidable presence.

We placed the collection on the table in the controlled atmosphere of the archive room and waited two days for the pages to absorb enough humidity that it would be safe to examine them under low light. Following each letter from the suitor was a thin sheet of paper in Isabella's hand. In keeping with the common practice of the times, she had made rough copies of her own letters before making the fair copy she would actually send.

The first letter from Isabella's suitor was signed with the initials H.H. The writer refers to "the old grudge between our families," just the clue we needed to identify him. The grudge had to be the feud that began when Josiah Pargeter lost his temper and struck Amos Hall with a turnip during the first winter, in 1833-34. When Ms. Cameron later checked the original listing of the MacNabb settlers on the Great Trek, she found among the Hall family members a certain "Hector, foundling boy adopted by the Halls on the wharf at Portnahaven." We also know that the first religious schism in Persephone was led by Amos Hall, who founded the New Congregational Church.

The letter goes on to mention a barn-raising on a farm belonging to one of the MacKelvey families on the Pine River, a great affair attended by many locals. The traditional climax of a barn-raising was the moment when the ridgepole was hoisted into position and the bravest of the young men climbed up and nailed a sprig of holly to it for luck. In this case, the young man was Hector Hall. As the crowd cheered, he tossed his cap into the air, and it sailed down to where Isabella was sitting and dropped in her lap. "You caught up my cap and beamed a smile at me that travelled straight to my heart," he confessed in his letter.

That night, judging from Isabella's reply, the young man crept down to the Pargeter barn on the edge of Larkspur and sang a gentle Gaelic song to his beloved as she milked the family cow. Suddenly the air was shattered by a blast from Josiah Pargeter's shotgun. Hector leapt over the hedge and disappeared into the woods. The next day Isabella wrote to him sternly, saying that "he was a wild and impertinent young man deserving of a good hiding," but then she relents and implores him "not to take such dangerous risks." In the margin of his letter she wrote out the verse of Hector's song and pressed the daisy chain he had woven for her between the pages.*

From here on, more tokens appear in the letters. There is a patch of homespun cloth with the third letter, a trophy hard won by Hector and his dog, Argus. It appears that one of Isabella's relatives had been alerted to the young man's interest in Isabella. The next night six of her male cousins lay in wait on Hall's Road as he came down the hill for another assignation in the stable. "As I emerged from

---

* "Oh, were my love yon lilac fair, / Wi' purple blossoms to the spring / And I a bird to shelter there / When wearied on my little wing."
– Robert Burns

the woods with Argus trotting at my heels, I was beset by a posse of attackers," Hector writes. "Even in the faint moonlight I recognized them as your kinsmen by their great hooked Pargeter noses." They fell upon him and would have beaten the daylights out of him if not for his faithful hound, which removed a large piece of one of his attackers' trousers – and the boys took to their heels. Hector kept his appointment with Isabella, and she lovingly pressed the patch of homespun between the pages of his letter. But she wrote back, scolding him for making "unseemly remarks about the Pargeter nose." If he "were so critical of a nose," she complained, then perhaps he "might look up in the highlands for some snub-nosed barefoot lass in a pigpen."

I chuckled as I read this. "Our Isabella is not a girl to be trifled with."

"Yes," agreed Ms. Cameron, adding, "that's the way the girls are in Persephone."

Hector now begged Isabella's forgiveness for the slight about the family nose and praised her own nose as "the straightest, sweetest nose on any face he had ever seen."

Isabella's next letter has water stains on it that, given its contents, can only have been caused by tears. Old Pargeter has confronted her with the news that she shall wed her cousin Fred MacKelvey, kinsman of the late Miller MacNabb. She describes Fred as "wheezing, stooped, and squinty-eyed," and tells Hector that the wedding is to take place in a week's time. Hector responds with a note urging her to run away with him and proposes a dramatic plan for their escape.

At this point, Ms. Cameron put her hand to her mouth and looked at me with wide eyes. I thought she must have left a pot burning on the stove at home.

"Wait," she said. "I'm sure I've read a newspaper story about this wedding. Just a minute . . ."

She jumped up and hurried to another part of the library. I caught up with her a few moments later and found her scrolling through microfilm files of the old *Free Press* newspaper. "There," she said triumphantly. "Look at this." On the screen was a page from the August 26, 1848, edition. Down the middle of the page was a single column with the title "Memorable Wedding." It was written by Homer Bell, the founding publisher and great-great-grandfather of the current owner of the *FP&E*, Edward Bell.*

Up until now in our story, the Bell family has had a muted presence in Persephone, busying itself with a combination of farming and blacksmithing. But the voice of the *Free Press* and its ruthless competitive practices soon brought the Bells into the front rank of the community's families.

"How could Homer Bell write all the gory details about something as sensitive as a disputed local wedding?" I asked.

"The Bells have always had the hide of a rhinoceros. I think that's how they've survived all these years running a newspaper in a small town."

As I looked over Ms. Cameron's shoulder, we read together.

MEMORABLE WEDDING
(The events at the recent Pargeter-MacKelvey wedding were sufficiently entertaining that they have displaced this week's chapter of the "The Princess and the Pirate," which will return to its usual space next week, readers take note.)
Residents of Larkspur found themselves at the eye of a matrimonial tempest on Saturday last, when

---

* Readers of Walt Wingfield's column will know him simply as "Ed."

Mr. and Mrs. Josiah Pargeter gave their only daughter Isabella in holy wedlock at the First Presbyterian Church.

The wedding was set for one o'clock, but a number of guests arrived earlier than expected. Chief among these was another suitor for Isabella's hand, Hector Hall, who had disguised himself as Dr. Ryan, the horseback preacher from Kempenfeldt, and made an attempt to carry Isabella from the side door of the church vestry, where the bride was preparing herself for the nuptials. Young Mr. Hall's bold plan might have succeeded were it not for the timely appearance of Isabella's father and about two dozen other male members of the clan. They immediately laid hands on Mr. Hall and dragged him back into the chancel area, where they proceeded to pummel him soundly. Hall fought back stoutly, and for a time it looked as though the little church would be kicked to kindling. But the genuine preacher, who had just arrived, waded into the fray and picked up Mr. Hall by what was left of his shirt and held him out of the reach of the flailing fists of his assailants. In a loud voice, the minister commanded them to cease fighting in the Lord's house. The room quieted down and Dr. Ryan lowered Mr. Hall. Suddenly, his attention was drawn to a small silver locket dangling at the lad's neck. With a cry, the man of God seized up this bauble with his free hand and examined it closely.

"Where did you get this locket, boy?" he demanded.

"I have worn it ever since the day I was pulled from the angry seas of the Middle Minch as a baby, you heathen b——. My father will swear to it!"

"Brother!" cried the minister. "You are saved!"

Dr. Ryan embraced Mr. Hall as tears of joy filled his eyes. Finally he held the confused young man at arm's length and announced to the amazed congregation:

"My family was lost at sea in the great blow of '32 in the Middle Minch. Father and Mother and my two sisters and the little brother I had never seen, all were drowned. They say that the captain and the first mate were arguing about transubstantiation and hit a rock. When I heard the news on the wharf at Belfast, I was struck down with grief and tore off my collar. I swore that I would never again serve only one church and contribute to the division of God's children on earth. And here is my mother's locket and my own dear brother, restored to me after all these years. The Lord's name be praised!"

"What is my name?" whispered Hector.

"You are Patrick Michael Ryan of County Down."

This announcement produced a great commotion in the church. For if young Mr. Hall's lost family was Catholic, how had his older brother acquired this charge in a Presbyterian church?

"It is true my beginnings were with the Church of Rome," explained Dr. Ryan. "But I have learned in my wanderings over the earth that there are many paths to Heaven. I now serve the Presbyterians, but I am often asked to do Methodists and Anglicans, and there's even a group of Zwinglians have asked me to visit up in Pluto Township."

"If I was born in the Catholic Church," said

Hector, "there's no place for me in this community. I am cast out on the waves once again."

The Pargeters and the MacKelveys and the other parishioners of First Presbyterian nodded their heads and agreed that he had summed up the situation very accurately.

"If she won't have me, there is none that will," cried Hector. And he turned to face his beloved, Isabella.

"I don't know, Hector," the young woman replied. "It's hard enough with the climate, the bugs, the work, and the bad food. I'm not sure if I can manage with the religious difference on top of it all."

At these harsh words, Hector flung himself out the door, leapt on his horse, and galloped off down the main street. His brother, the minister, watched him go and said tenderly, "He's young. He'll get over it. In time he will learn that it is better to have loved and lost than to have loved and won." He turned back to the congregation. "So shall we proceed with the wedding?"

Fred MacKelvey stepped forward to the altar, but Isabella Pargeter held up her hand.

"I'm not taking that one," she said firmly. "And if you think I am, you can all sit down and have another good think."

Old Josiah Pargeter now spoke up. "Perhaps I have been a bit harsh," he said. "When we crossed the ocean we agreed to put all the old quarrels behind us. This land is hard enough without putting neighbour against neighbour over small matters. Mr. MacKelvey, let us step outside and talk some business."

Our readers will be pleased to hear that after some negotiation between the two families, a wedding did take place. Isabella Pargeter was united in matrimony with Fred's older brother Alexander MacKelvey, who has better eyesight and not even a trace of a stoop.

The bride was radiant in an empire gown trimmed with lace and a nosegay of fragrant wildflowers. Her niece Rosemary charmed the assembly as flower girl. The floral arrangements in the church were particularly lovely, drawing from the late summer gardens of both families . . .

The newspaper account came to a close with the report that an elders' meeting followed the service, and the leaders of the church agreed to advertise for a new minister as soon as possible.

Ms. Cameron and I turned back to the packet of love letters from the hope chest. The last one is on plain white paper, dated one year later and postmarked from Australia.

Dear Isabella:
After arduous travels and many adventures, my long-lost brother and I have found a green hill in Kookaburra that reminds me of Hall's Hill in the forest of Upper Canada. He has a small parish here with the New Reformed Church of New South Wales, and I am getting along by raising sheep.

No matter how long I live, I will always remember the hills of Persephone and the girl I left behind in Larkspur.

My best wishes to you for happiness in this life,
Hector

Enclosed in this last letter was a silver trinket about the size of my thumbnail. I opened it carefully and read aloud the Gaelic inscription. "Boie yuhd, ma vourneen!"* I heard a sniff and looked over at Ms. Cameron. She was dabbing at her eyes with a tissue.

"It's Hector's locket," I said. She nodded.

I patted her hand and we sat for a moment together, thinking about lost love and the sadness of it all. Then we tied up the letters and put them into a manila envelope that we marked "Hector and Isabella." Ms. Cameron looked in the trunk and pulled out a heavy brown folder. She unwound from the two buttons the string that held it together.

"Hmm," she said, peeking inside. "Deeds."

She drew out a handful of legal papers that documented the transfer of the MacNabb properties to Alexander "Big Sandy" MacKelvey in 1850. There were the two mills, the store, and several farms and houses. The inventory lists included mortgages held on other farms and businesses in the township.

"Good heavens," I said. "It looks like Big Sandy got the whole pile."

"And Isabella took financial security in exchange for a loveless marriage. That would explain the bottle collection in the attic."

"He was MacNabb's nephew, but he still had to jump through some hoops to prove his uncle's death," said Ms. Cameron.

She showed me a letter dated January 10, 1850, from the provincial registrar, certifying the death of Alexander MacNabb and approving the will for probate.

* "Victory to you, my darling!"

Enclosed with the letter was a bill from a stonemason for the carving of a headstone. Apparently the bill had been challenged and the amount crossed out several times, the amount decreasing each time. Further down, the dates 1781-1846 were noted, along with several drafts of the proposed wording for the engraving. Again, some unknown editor had stroked out every suggestion except the last one; "Laird MacNabb," "Chief of the Clan MacNabb," "Founder of the Glen Islet Settlement" had all been rejected.

The final entry was the one I had discovered in the cemetery only a few weeks before. Below it was a cryptic scribble: "You made it look like we killed him ourselves. I'm not paying for this. Let the millstone be his monument! A. MacKelvey."

"There it is. Alexander Lachlan MacNabb, Miller of Hollyhock. They were the same person after all," said Doreen.

"There was no conspiracy," I said. "Just a botched engraving job, and Big Sandy wouldn't approve it."

So ended our quest for the resting place of the Laird or Miller MacNabb, not with a bang but with a whimper. As my grandfather observes in his preface, "When the historian is presented with a choice between Conspiracy and Chaos, it is always safer to assume that Chaos is responsible for the mischief."

We locked the door of the library archives and strolled up Wellington Street to the Red Hen Restaurant for a late supper. The scent of purple lilacs, those sturdy shrubs planted so long ago by the pioneers, perfumed the still evening air. As we walked, I sang a verse of an old Australian folk song:

Oh had I the flight of the bronzewing
Far over the plains would I fly,
Straight to the land of my childhood
And there I would lay down and die . . .

Wood-burning steam locomotives like this one opened up Persephone to even greater exploitation by outsiders. Great fortunes were made in the construction of the railroads, although very little of the wealth stayed in Persephone. But the promise of easy riches distracted many farmers and set the stage for financial catastrophe.

Chapter 5

THE COMING OF THE RAILWAY
1850 TO 1859

———————•◦•◦•———————

P eople think of pioneer days as having lasted through most of the nineteenth century and as a time when people lived in isolated log cabins, made their own soap from wood ashes, and stirred up the soil between the stumps with primitive plows pulled by teams of emaciated oxen. In reality, such scenes vanished from most southern Ontario communities within a decade of settlement as scores of newcomers arrived, cleared whole tracts of wilderness, and set up bustling communities at every crossroads.

Thanks to a clever bit of research of my own, I have been able to fix the end of Persephone's pioneer days at exactly mid-century. As evidence I submit the special Progress Edition of the Larkspur *Free Press* of June 17, 1850. This issue is referred to in the minutes of the Larkspur Town Council – the town was incorporated the same year, with Big Sandy MacKelvey serving as clerk – but my research associate could turn up no trace of it in the newspaper archives. She assumed it had been destroyed by one of the many fires set during the Newspaper Wars. However, I discovered it in the most surprising place: hanging in a glass frame on the wall of the front office of the *Free Press & Economist*, only a few yards from Ms. Cameron's desk. I suppose it's been there so long, people just stopped looking at it.

In those days, with little capital at stake and relying entirely on weekly sales and advertising revenues for profit, these publications could afford to be strident, sensational, and mud-slinging, unlike newspapers today.

According to the Progress Edition of June 1850, Larkspur had grown into a bustling community of twenty-five hundred people. Editor Homer Bell proudly announced the figure in a banner headline, followed by a wildly optimistic leader on the community's future prospects: "At the present rate of growth, we confidently predict that Larkspur will some day eclipse its rival Toronto and stand with London, Paris, and other great urban centres . . ." Homer had it half right. Larkspur does indeed stand shoulder to shoulder with Paris, Warsaw, Athens, Moscow, and many other small Ontario towns today.

Two long rows of storefronts, two churches, and a town hall lined the town's respectable main thoroughfare, Wellington Street. The paper carried advertisements for five blacksmith shops, four hotels, two dry goods merchants, two hardware stores, the MacKelvey mills, a brickworks, two shoemakers, four barber shops, two bakeries, and the Larkspur Distillery, now housed in a brick building at the base of Mill Street on the old battlefield site in front of MacNabb's store.

In the countryside surrounding Larkspur, the landscape had been transformed. The forest wall had been pushed back several miles in each direction. Dusty roads crisscrossed the Pine River plain, where snake rail fences enclosed field after field of waving wheat and grazing cattle. Up on the drumlins, stump fences did a reasonable job of impeding the movement of sheep and goats, although the concept of a fence was rooted in the idea that it should keep livestock out rather than in.

Big Sandy MacKelvey had a firm hand on the tiller of commerce, as owner of the mills, the distillery, and the brickworks. Colonel Fortescue, now approaching sixty, had gained control of vast tracts of the Petunia Valley timber-lands, through his close ties with the government and the Anglican Church. He also held mortgages with so many of the farmers that in 1847 he founded the Persephone Bank in offices in the Commercial Block on Wellington Street.

Dr. Goulding makes an interesting observation about this new era in the opening to his chapter on mid-Victorian life in the township: "Here we see the township in the full glory of the Jeffersonian ideal. The countryside yielded up the bounty of its fields to the residents of Larkspur, who returned the favour by supplying sturdy homemade iron implements, bricks, and planks for the industrious hus-bandman and importing small luxuries for his wife such as tea, sugar, soap, and British cloth. The teeming, huddled masses who made the perilous journey across the Atlantic had in fifteen short years thrown off the heavy yoke of poverty and oppression and now enjoyed a steady diet of potatoes and pork in front of a blazing hearth they could call their own."

In the above passage I catch a glimmer of the Michael Bliss paradigm, the idea that Persephone is a land of limited opportunity where smart people, content with modest returns for hard work and a willingness to share the common wealth, had thrown off the yoke of poverty and oppression.

The picture my grandfather paints of that healthy young community is actually quite attractive, and it gave me a little pang of regret to think of how far short it has fallen of its own expectations. It made me wonder what spell was cast on Persephone to reduce its state of affairs so drastically. How did it move from a vigorous, confident, and self-reliant place to the sleepy backwater it is today?

Part of the answer is that, for some people, progress in Persephone wasn't coming nearly fast enough.

By 1850, the only people left making their own soap in an outdoor kettle and weaving cloth on their own looms were the Haddocks and the Smarts, perched on their view property on the edge of the Great Rift. The thirteen years since the abortive rebellion must have been difficult ones. Archie had banished himself all the way to the Far East, and Adelaide's repeated attempts to contact him with the news that he was not on the list of rebels produced no response. However, his letters to Adelaide had come regularly from a string of ports on the Pacific Rim, where he served on various ships and eventually found a position advising a Chinese warlord on the use of explosives. When Adelaide's letters finally caught up with him in 1842, he had taken his time making his way home.

While the rest of their neighbours made plans to build brick farmhouses and convert the original log shanties to pig sheds, Fanny Haddock dreamed of a real plank floor for the kitchen of her ramshackle cabin. Her husband, Bertram, still spent much of his time either hunting squirrels for the pot or staring glass-eyed at the wall. He'd been working on chopping down his second tree for eight years, and as yet the farm amounted to little more than a large garden. Some people are meant to be pioneers; Bertram Haddock wasn't one of them. If it hadn't been for the small annuities that Fanny and Adelaide received from home, both families would have been destitute. In the meantime, the sisters took refuge in each other's company, while tending to their growing brood of children.

One day in the middle of 1846, Archie suddenly showed up in the laneway, tanned and fit after his years on the lam, and with enough money to buy a cleared farm two miles further up the road. In 1847, he, Adelaide, and their son George Gordon (now twelve) moved out of the Haddock cabin they had moved into "for a few weeks, until we get settled" twelve years before.

Archie Smart was certainly more ambitious than Bertram Haddock, but his exile had made him impatient with the drudgery of farm work. Before long, he too tired of the daily chores. When the rebels of 1837 were finally granted a general amnesty, he took a position as ordnance officer with the Petunia Valley Foot Regiment, still commanded by Fortescue. He could often be found down at the McQuarrie Quarries experimenting with his first love, blasting powder.

A mere two miles now separated the sisters, but they communicated by sweet-talking the driver of the mail cart that passed their cabins. Fanny and Adelaide made their threadbare lives tolerable by putting on entertainments for the neighbours who gradually took up residence on the remaining lots on the road running along the edge of the Great Rift, all the decent land in the township having by now been cleared and settled. These were a horny-handed lot, most of whom had no formal schooling, and they must have been puzzled to sit on log benches in the clearing, watching as Fanny and Adelaide and their families acted out "The Fall of Carthage and the Death of Queen Dido" and other classically inspired dramatic works. The sisters wrote all their own material and taught each of their children to play an instrument. Bertram made twig furniture for the sets and Archie handled the lighting and sound effects. In idle moments Adelaide could often be seen sketching in the woods, although she had to be content with natural materials like birchbark and vegetable dyes because she couldn't afford real artists' supplies. Unfortunately, little of her work has come down to us. The sisters were both determined to maintain "the gentle arts of music, literature, and poetry" as a bulwark against the rough ways of the Ontario countryside.

Two characters who had far less reason to be dissatisfied with their lots in life than the Haddocks and Smarts were pressing hard to improve their fortunes. The old alliance between Charles Augustus Fortescue and Alexander MacNabb had dissolved under MacNabb's successor, Big Sandy MacKelvey. In the 1850 Progress Edition, there are signs of a spirited rivalry between the twin captains of finance and commerce. One ad for the Persephone Bank urges residents to "avoid usurious credit charges at the local mills and stores" by seeking "affordable" mortgages from the bank. On the same page, MacKelvey fires back with a warning to "avoid the clutches of finance companies" with their "punishing rates of interest and predatory practices in recovering loans." The two men had built large brick houses at opposite ends of Wellington Street in Larkspur.

Homer Bell's editorial in the same edition of the *Free Press* gives his own pointed advice about the way forward for Larkspur: "What is needed to complete this happy picture of prosperity and confirm for all time the bright prospects of our fair community is, of course, a railway line from Kempenfeldt through Larkspur to the Bay. In laying this new line, the railway builders will only be confirming in steel what the ancient peoples of North America have known for centuries: that Larkspur stands at a natural crossroads to the Northwest."* This editorial seems to be the earliest reference in the community to what soon became known as the northern railway.

Persephone's enthusiasm for the railway age came at one of the worst moments in the history of the popular nineteenth-century sport of railway financing and building. In 1847 the railway investment bubble had popped in England, following which all sources of financing dried up like a farm pond in late August. In its aftermath, railway stockholders around the globe finally twigged to the fact that trains were so expensive to build and so difficult to manage that almost none of them made a profit for anyone but the promoters and the contractor. Steamboats made money because you didn't have to build a roadbed for them. Wagon traffic made money because horses and wagon wheels were cheap to replace and could cover rough ground. The trains were fast and offered great convenience, but they ate up private fortunes at a rate that even a notorious spendthrift like the Duke of Marlborough found sobering. By the time the *Free Press* editorial was being read by the citizens of Persephone, private money had all but vanished from the railway business.

The editor of the *Free Press* did make a valid point. The ancient peoples of Ontario had been crossing the township on footpaths along the edges of the Petunia River Valley for many centuries. What he forgot to mention was that most of the ancient people who passed through Larkspur were

* This observation on transportation policy was the first and only time the *Free Press* strayed from the three editorial themes that have carried it through the last century and a half: the incompetence of the post office, the idiocy of governments, and the urgent need to abolish school boards.

actually on their way to somewhere else. If they did stop, it was usually to ask for directions, the way people stop today at Ron's Service Station at the corner of Wellington and Mill Streets.

With or without investment capital, Canadian promoters regularly announced grandiose new railway projects. Every year, private bills were introduced in the provincial legislature for new railway companies going every which way. But by mid-century, only one of them had been built: a rickety little track fourteen miles long that went west out of Montreal and bypassed the Lachine Rapids. It deserves mention for two reasons: it was the first railway in the Canadas to make money – and it was the last.

It is difficult to hold the attention of the average reader for more than a few minutes on the subject of Canadian railways before the eyes glaze over and the forehead comes to rest on the page. There are only two things you need to know about Canadian railway building. If the route goes north-south and crosses the border to the United States, it was probably built by businessmen. If it goes east-west and doesn't cross the border, it was built by politicians.

Time and again, promoters suggested a northern railway to link Lake Ontario to Georgian Bay and the shipping route to the Upper Great Lakes. Time after time, the proposal fell victim to the jostling of special interests, the lack of available capital, and the inability of the promoters to agree on the path the railway would take. The most favoured route to Georgian Bay travelled north of Toronto to Kempenfeldt, then went straight on up the Old Military Road, or Fortunes of War Road, to Penetanguishene Harbour. I say "favoured" because the old soldiers who owned the land on both sides of the road were well connected and carried considerable influence in the provincial capital. But its strategic position as a naval harbour put Penetang a long way from the main shipping lanes of the upper lakes. No offence intended to the citizens of that lovely port town, but this route was a railway to nowhere.

Ever the visionary, Charles Fortescue had breathed life into the railway debate by calling for the establishment of a new port city on the lakeshore north of Larkspur, at the mouth of the Petunia River. His plan called for a railway line from Toronto to Kempenfeldt that would then hike west across Demeter before it descended to the lake following the Petunia River Valley. Fortescue's route might involve a few more miles of roadbed than the Penetang route, but its terminus would be much closer to Lake Huron.

Fortescue seems to have believed that Persephone needed to become a destination in its own right, rather than just another portage route. So he proposed that the new town of Port Petunia, as he intended to christen it, would be a shipbuilding centre manufacturing lake boats to serve the growing traffic from the bay to the Upper Great Lakes. He saw how the Petunia Valley line would connect Toronto to Chicago and the booming American west, how the shipyards would thrive on the increased traffic, how wheat, wood, and fish would go south and manufactured goods, food, and textiles would travel north and west to where they were needed most, in the remote outposts of the frontier. He also grasped that even if none of the above occurred, he personally stood to make a pile of money selling land and building lots along the Petunia Valley route.

It was a far-sighted plan – if the closest you'd ever come to visiting Persephone was trying to locate it on a government topographical map. For those on the scene, the view was not so rosy. Take, for example, the owners of the thirty-nine taverns along the New Military Road to Persephone. One look at Fortescue's planned railway told them the Petunia Valley route spelled business disaster. If you could make the trip from Toronto to Port Petunia in three hours, you wouldn't have to spend the night at any of the hostelries along the way. Nor would you need the services of the many teamsters who hauled freight along the road. Ship captains were also opposed to the idea of a port at this location, noting the exposed nature of the site and the hazardous approach through the Hawk and Hatchling Islands, so named because of the way their treacherous shoals preyed on passing ships. There was also the terrific pressure of the ice that blows down the lake in spring and piles up on shore, grinding everything in its path like a miniature glacier. But the greatest flaw in Fortescue's route, from Larkspur's point of view, was that the line bypassed the village.

The absence of private financing seemed to make any rail scheme in British North America a complete pipe dream. But one night in 1849, Charles Fortescue sat straight up in bed and shouted, "I have it! The money will come from the taxpayers!" He made this entry in large black letters underlined in the third volume of his scrapbook and dashed off for Toronto in his carriage to see Francis Hincks, a prominent politician and railway promoter who would in due course become premier of the United Province of Upper and Lower Canada. Fortescue had hit upon his greatest inspiration, an innovation that would ultimately provide others with the creative spark needed to build a truly national transportation network and show the way for generations of Canadian entrepreneurs. Hincks and his associates heard out the Colonel's plan to resurrect the northern railway and lay a hundred miles of track from

Toronto to a new port city that would rise on the south-western shore of Georgian Bay.

My grandfather's extensive collection of hardcover books, which he left to the Larkspur library, includes the memoirs of an old judge and long-time civil servant of the province, J.P. Ridout: *Reflections on Pioneer Life and Customs in Upper Canada, 1874*, now out of print.* Ridout, who belonged to Hincks's inner circle, gives us a first-hand account of this meeting. He describes how the politician listened patiently to Fortescue as the promoter explained the merits of the Petunia Valley route. Eventually, Hincks interrupted with a question.

> "We have been discussing the possibility of such a railway down at the British Coffee House on York Street since 1834. How do you expect to raise the sum of $2.5 million at a time when railway stock certificates are being used to house-train puppies and line birdcages?"
>
> "How do you get four elephants into a stage-coach?" countered Fortescue.
>
> There was a brief startled silence. The Colonel paused dramatically before leaning forward and pounding his fist on the polished table.
>
> "You put two in the front seat and two in the back! That is how we will finance this railway, gentlemen. The government of the Province will guarantee half the cost, and the City of Toronto and the county governments at both ends will raise $200,000 each from the property tax base. The rest will come

---

* As far as I can tell, the library possesses the only copy, the others having been burned as part of an out-of-court settlement in a salacious divorce proceeding.

from the railway contractor. In two years, the first railway in Canada will connect Lake Ontario, Lake Simcoe, and Lake Huron."*

"Brilliant," breathed Hincks wonderingly. "The man is a genius."†

The Colonel spent the next year patiently lobbying provincial and local politicians. But when he learned that a rival company was beginning work on an east-west rail line that would connect Montreal to Toronto, he redoubled his efforts. The competing plan would push on west and forge a direct link between the St. Lawrence River and Chicago across southern Ontario. Fortescue realized it was now or never for his dream of a northern line.

In no time he assembled the commitments of the three governments and an American railway contractor, but agents for the Fortunes of War route were also active. During one of Fortescue's frequent business trips out of the township, promoters of this rival route agitated with the teamsters and tavernkeepers who made their living from the passing traffic on the New Military Road. Before long, opinion in the township had swung against the Petunia Valley route. The leading voice raised against it was none other than that of Big Sandy MacKelvey of Larkspur. In a large paid advertisement that appeared in the *Free Press* on June 15, 1851, MacKelvey swore that he would never pay "a penny of tax to support a scheme that promises to take the

---

* Fortescue was conveniently omitting the money-making Lachine railway.

† This is one of the earliest examples of a public-private partnership in Ontario.

bread off the plates of my neighbours and customers." The *Free Press* itself, in a sudden reversal of its pro-railway editorial policy, thundered: "Not a penny of tribute to the railway promoters and their lackeys in Toronto!" The town council of Larkspur promptly passed a resolution rejecting the plan.

Finally Fortescue's financing was in place. York and Simcoe Counties meekly agreed to subscribe their shares of $200,000, as did the City of Toronto. Each received that amount in stock certificates in the new Ontario, Simcoe, and Huron Railway. The contractor ponied up $500,000, and a few private investors like Sir Allan Napier MacNab, leader of the Tory party, and C.A. Fortescue provided the rest. It had all been surprisingly easy – perhaps too easy.

Colonel Fortescue was the only resident of Persephone Township who stood to benefit from the Petunia Valley route, and unfortunately for him, the as yet imaginary citizens of Port Petunia could not vote. The first warden of the newly incorporated Simcoe County, Jacob Aemilius Irving (known to later generations as the Father of Euchre), announced that all the townships of Simcoe, including Persephone, would share equally in the railway investment and reap the rewards accordingly. Then he announced that property taxes would rise by one-third. When the townships on the western fringe of Simcoe, which stood at the greatest distance from the proposed line, heard this news, they rebelled. On the night of August 25, 1851, the municipal leaders of the townships of Mono, Mulmur, Osprey, Artemisia, Euthanasia, Persephone, Demeter, and Pluto converged on the Larkspur Town Hall in a public meeting to organize a tax revolt.

Homer Bell of the *Free Press* wrote a report on that meeting.

The crowd that filled the hall in the stifling heat of the
late summer evening was peevish and clamorous. No
speaker who took the floor could hold it for more than
a moment before he was drowned out by angry inter-
ruptions. Everyone insisted on speaking at once. After
a time, Big Sandy MacKelvey, the clerk of Larkspur
Town Council and a prominent businessman of the
Town, strode to the stage where he stood unspeaking,
waiting for quiet. It is said that Mr. MacKelvey can
still lift a barrel of Larkspur whisky above his head, a
feat which earns him the respect of many of his fellow
councillors, who can raise the whisky only in smaller
quantities, as far as their chins.

When the room fell silent, he spoke in the gentle
burr of his native Glen Islet. "My friends, we can
shout at each other all night and it will nae change
the price of potatoes in the morning. If we hae bread
on the table and hay in our barns, it is because we
ken the value of an honest day's work. The railway
men ken no such law. They would hae you think
you can make a hoose out of straw and spin a fine
coat from horsehair. We hae seen their like before.
The Conservative land grabbers of the past have
become the railway plunderers of the present. They
are like the warble flies that burrow into your cattle
and feed off them for the winter. In the spring they
will be fat and fly away, leavin' their hosts skinny
and sick. But not if you refuse to feed 'em. I say not
a penny of our taxes to these railway men and their
lackeys in Toronto!"

The crowd erupted in a cheer. When Mr.
MacKelvey sat down, the Reeve of Euthanasia
Township stood and announced a resolution to secede

from Simcoe County and declare independence. One by one the Reeves of the other seven townships rose to support him.*

According to Bell's *Free Press* report, which Ms. Cameron turned up in her preliminary searches, this was the end of the meeting. But just before this book was ready to go to press, she discovered a clipping from the *Expositor*, one of the rival Larkspur papers. As far as I can tell, it is the only surviving evidence that this newspaper actually existed. Ms. Cameron found it attached to a repair bill for damages to the meeting hall in the township accounts for that fall. The clipping picks up where the *Free Press* left off.

As Clerk MacKelvey sat down, Colonel Charles Augustus Fortescue, Chairman of the Persephone Bank, Director of the Petunia Valley Railway Action Committee, and a prominent landowner in that township, who had so far sat silently through the proceedings, rose to challenge him. In full dress uniform of the Petunia Valley Foot Regiment, wearing his medals and sword, he struck a martial pose worthy of the Iron Duke, his old commander.

"In three years," said Fortescue, "you will have a market for your fat cattle and sheep, three hours away in Toronto. Your farms will triple in value, and your children will bathe regularly and learn to play the piano. Do not let backwardness and woolly thinking block the way forward. The railway must come to Persephone!"

---

* Most of these townships eventually formed the new counties of Dufferin and Grey.

A noisome crowd of Demeter farmers, most likely holders of property along the proposed Petunia Valley route, raised a great cheer in support of Fortescue.

"But what if we can't pay the taxes? Shall we lose our farms?" shouted a voice from Pluto. An angry murmur ran through the assembly and a scuffle broke out in front of the platform.

Colonel Fortescue drew his sword and held it up in the air for all to see. "This is the sword I used at Queenston Heights. I carved Persephone Township out of the woods with this sword before many of you were born, and I am not about to fly away like one of Big Sandy's warble flies. You have the word of an officer."

Modern-day politicians have learned not to hold contentious public meetings in Persephone during the late summer, when there is a surplus of fruit and vegetables in the countryside, especially those varieties that do not keep well in warm weather. Given the combustible nature of emotions in the hall, it should have surprised no one when the first tomato flew through the air and exploded on the wall behind the Colonel. The Colonel waved his sword defiantly in the air, shouting, "To me! Men of Demeter! To me!" Then he jumped down off the platform and made for the side door.

The farmers of Demeter surged forward and seized Fortescue, whose primary intent seems to have been to get himself rescued. They carried him on their shoulders out through the main doors and down the steps of the town hall in a hail of soft cucumbers and overripe pears. From the safety of his carriage in the street, and protected by a ring of his supporters, Fortescue turned and shouted at the sullen crowd now pouring out of the hall.

"The railway is coming to Persephone whether you like it or not. You will all rue the day you stood in the way of the Petunia Valley route. I'll make grass grow here in the streets of Larkspur, and I will pave the streets of Port Petunia with gold." Then he drove off.

After the meeting broke up, Big Sandy and his wife, Isabella, strolled home together. In a rare moment of domestic felicity, Big Sandy took his wife's arm and spoke to her from his heart. He knew that though the townships' battle for independence might be won, the fight to keep the railway out of Persephone was futile. Fortescue's dream of a thriving port on Georgian Bay had captured the imagination of the Toronto politicians. Nothing could now prevent it from becoming a reality.

I have been able to recreate this intimate scene thanks to a rough copy of a letter found in Isabella's hope chest, written to her sister soon after the events at the town hall.

"That a railway cannot make a profit and sucks the savings out of every township it passes through is not enough to stop its being built," she quoted her husband as telling her. "And when it is built, Larkspur will fade from the scene just as surely as the evening star will fade from the sky tomorrow morning. It cannot be helped."

As the couple walked under the young maple trees that lined both sides of Wellington Street, they saw old Duncan MacKeown, the faithful lamplighter of Larkspur, trudging along, dousing the gas lamps. Isabella's letter concludes on an elegiac note: "As we were nearing Islet Cottage, I turned to Big Sandy, whose face looked softer than I had seen it since the day we were married. 'We must prepare ourselves,' he sighed, 'for hard times if we are to stay in Larkspur.'"

Just as Big Sandy MacKelvey had predicted, the refusal of Persephone and the other rebel townships to participate in the railway's financing hardly slowed the project. The government took no action against the tax revolt in the northwest, allowing all the rebel townships to operate independently of Simcoe County for the time being. But the route for the railway after it reached Kempenfeldt remained undecided. Fortescue took matters into his own hands and announced that he would purchase a right-of-way without consulting any municipal leader in Persephone or Demeter, immediately causing the price of every piece of flat ground along both sides of the Petunia River to triple.

The first shovel went into the ground for the Ontario, Simcoe, and Huron Railway on September 10, 1851, on Front Street in Toronto, at a vice-regal sod-turning attended by the governor general and his wife, Lord and Lady Elgin. Lady Elgin wielded the miniature silver spade, and she placed a small pile of dirt into an exquisite little hardwood wheelbarrow.

Dr. Goulding offers this wry comment on the significance of the moment in the conclusion to his chapter on the railway building era in Persephone: "A tiny shovelful of dirt marked the beginning of a half-century of self-dealing, nest-feathering, public-purse-snatching, and lying that would become the hallmarks of Canadian railway building and give us dozens of new mansions in Montreal, Toronto, and Chicago."

Whenever you take on a building project in rural Ontario today, farmers will pull in off the road moments after the backhoe arrives to tell you that you're putting the house, the garage, or the swimming pool in the wrong place. They've always done this and I have no explanation for it. It appears this tradition was already well established in 1852. As the railway crews moved north from Toronto into the hills of King Township, the skeptics warned that the grade would be too steep. At the Holland Marsh, people shook their heads and warned that a track could not be built across a bog. By now the crews were slicing through the farmland at the rate of $50,000 a mile, which was almost twice as much as the most optimistic hopes of the contractor. As workers laid the track, they also sank poles beside the line and hung the first telegraph wires.

In the summer of 1853, the railway reached Kempenfeldt just as the contractor discovered that the funds from the debentures were completely exhausted. He fired off a message to his employers, the first telegram to be sent from Simcoe County, a triumphant message announcing, "Railway finished!" This was duly handed on to Premier Hincks.

"Finished?" the premier cabled back. "What about connection to Georgian Bay?"

"Our mistake," replied the contractor. "Company finished. No money left."

This pioneering electronic exchange is preserved in the restored Station House Museum in Port Petunia.

The government in Toronto can be forgiven its bewilderment. It had no direct experience of the complex world of railway financing. Here was a situation that railway men understood much better than the ordinary layman who understands only the workings of regular business. When there is no money left in a railway project, the railway man instinctively knows it is time to pack his trunk and leave town to search for somewhere else to build a railway. The only argument that can persuade him to stay is the news that the government is willing to assist in a "reorganization" of the company.

The first reorganization of the Ontario, Simcoe, and Huron occurred just as the first train sounded its whistle and steamed out of the Front Street Station destined for Bradford, thirty miles north of the city, on May 16, 1853. The *Toronto*, the first engine built in Canada, pulled two coaches and a freight car carrying a cargo of tea, a dozen brooms, and a bag of salt. The company had advertised that clergymen would be allowed to ride free. Remarkably enough, every single one of the seventy-three passengers on that first train presented himself as a man of the cloth.

The government poured fresh funds into the revamped company while the debate over the optimum route north to Georgian Bay resumed. No fewer than four different routes were now proposed, each one having its own set of advantages and disadvantages.

Fortescue's route along the Petunia River through Demeter Township was probably the best from a construction point of view, being mostly over flat and solid ground. However, it wasn't until the directors of the railway company paid the contractor a bribe of somewhere between $15,000 and $20,000 out of the government rescue package that common sense prevailed. The crews immediately pointed their survey equipment in the direction of Port Petunia, which was taking shape under the command of the former surveyor. The Colonel had marked out a complete town site west of the rail line and sold lots as fast as he could have the deeds printed.

In his railway promotion literature, Fortescue had described his rising port city as the "Chicago of the North." Now that it was time to lay out the streets and make the town ready for settlement, he took a street map of Chicago, turned it sideways, and superimposed it on the shoreline of Georgian Bay. This is why the main street of Port Petunia is called Michigan Avenue and the baseball park was later called Wrigley Field. The farmers of Persephone shook their heads wonderingly when they saw that a horse-drawn streetcar line was slated to cross the shale beach and the cedar swamps to connect their shanties to the Grand Central Hotel. (Fortunately, this scheme of Fortescue's never got off the drawing board.) By the time the railroad builders started pushing west from Kempenfeldt, there were five hundred houses under construction in Port Petunia, nine taverns, three houses of horizontal refreshment, two newspapers, and a racetrack, and there was some talk of building a church.

In the fall of 1854, the tracks reached the bay. It was an excellent roadbed, with a solid foundation of limestone rocks and washed gravel from the Petunia River. The line still exists, almost the only surviving remnant of the spider-web of railways that once covered this part of southern Ontario. Travellers who take the train to Port Petunia today, and there are very few of those, wonder why the track makes so many twists and turns across the flats of the Petunia River Valley. The answer? The landowners of the 1850s set such high prices on their properties that Fortescue had to deviate from the customary straight line to find an affordable route.

In June 1855, the first train steamed into Port Petunia, carrying all the dignitaries of the Ontario, Simcoe, and Huron board of directors, the entire cabinet of the United Province, and another fifty or sixty clergymen, aides-de-camp, executive assistants, and lesser lords and attendants. The new Port Petunia *Gleaner* newspaper made a great fuss that the cargo of brooms delivered numbered well over a dozen and reported: "The crowd repaired to the newly opened Port Petunia Grand Central Hotel and drank the health of the bondholders who had so generously under-written all this great fun. When the whistle finally sounded at sunset, they supported each other back to the waiting train and steamed off south to Toronto."

From Hall's Hill, Homer Bell, the editor of the Larkspur *Free Press*, stood with a small crowd of local people, watching the little train puffing away across Demeter Township. Big Sandy MacKelvey turned to him and said gruffly: "It is a long road that does nae bend. Two can play at this game."

The next day Big Sandy set out on horseback to Hamilton, where officials of the rival Grand Trunk Railway were making plans to extend the route west across the Ontario heartland to Chicago, thus besting the northern railway, whose freight had to travel much of the way by ship. In large part thanks to his efforts, the Grand Trunk decided to build a feeder line to Port Petunia from Hamilton, passing through Larkspur before it pushed on to the north. They were none too soon. By that time, Larkspur's population had dwindled to a fraction of its 1850 size, having lost most of its numbers to Port Petunia and Demeter Centre, a new town that sprang up six miles to the east on Fortescue's railway line. The Algonquin Railway would give Larkspur a last-minute reprieve from oblivion. But I'm getting ahead of my story.

The northern railway to Port Petunia was incorporated as the Ontario, Simcoe, and Huron Inland Transportation Co. Too late it was realized that the acronym could not be used on the letterhead, because it came too close to express-ing the feelings of the debenture holders upon learning that the company would not be paying a dividend at any time in the foreseeable future. In polite company it became known as the Fast Freight.

Big Sandy's line through Larkspur, when it finally

arrived, would be considerably slower, chugging up through the drumlins at a top speed of about eighteen miles an hour and stopping whenever anyone flagged it down to load an animal or a bag of grain or even waved at it. The Algonquin soon became known as the Hog Special. The Port Petunia *Gleaner* sneered that "Larkspur's little engines require no cowcatcher at the front, because they do not travel fast enough to overtake a cow. The chief risk from livestock roaming free on the roadbed is that cattle do sometimes climb on the back of the Hog Special and move among the passengers, creating a disturbance which is objectionable."

From her perch high on the Great Rift, Adelaide Smart observed the progress of Colonel Fortescue's railway along the Petunia Valley and concluded that she and her son, George Gordon, had had enough. After twenty years in the highlands, more than a decade of it living in a ménage à trois with her sister, Fanny, and Fanny's morose husband, Bertram, while Archie served out his self-imposed banishment on the other side of the world, Adelaide had precious little to show for her labours. The food on her table came from two cows in the barn and a large garden, but the farm itself produced nothing in the way of income. Archie had given up planting wheat and was now spending most of his spare time, which was a lot of time, in the billiards room of the new Grand Central Hotel in Port Petunia. From the window over her dry sink, Adelaide had an unobstructed view of the new town on the lake. The Westerlies howled against the shanty walls for months on end. For years she had been content to while away the winters, stitching her embroidered tablecloths that told the story of the Pilgrim's Progress, sketching scenes of drumlin life, corresponding with her sister, and entertaining the children with her legends of the Irish chieftain Chuchulain. Now her annuity had run out, and she had to face the hard reality that it was time to find an occupation that produced some cash.

Fortunately, salvation miraculously appeared. Archie had applied for the position of postmaster for the new town of Port Petunia when it separated from the township in 1855. As a former junior officer in Wellington's army, he had by far the most impressive resumé among the numerous applicants. His successful application helped launch a long and distinguished Persephone tradition: achieving success after years of penury by means of a government appointment. In the fall of that year, Adelaide and Archie loaded their possessions into a wagon and without a backward glance drove away from the farm they'd cleared. Two weeks before Christmas they took up residence in a small frame house on Illinois Street, just west of the railway station.

One of Adelaide Smart's first projects was the founding of the Terpsichore (rhymes with "hickory" if you're from south of Highway 401; in Port Petunia, it is pronounced "Turps-core") Society, a group devoted to fostering the dramatic arts.* Adelaide could not contain her joy when she wrote to her sister: "Dearest Fanny, We are delivered, just as surely as the Israelites were safely guided through the perils of the desert. I am so delighted to be off that barren cliff and returned to the joys of Civilization. I have noisy neighbours I can see out my windows on each side, and the clatter of traffic on the street lulls me to sleep at night."

Fanny wrote back, rejoicing at her sister's good fortune and bravely putting her own desperate situation aside with an attempt at humour. "My dear Addle-pated Addie, Your

---

* Terpsichore was the Greek muse of lyric poetry, interpretive dance, figure skating, and curling. She is often portrayed tied into a theatre seat, wearing an agonized expression.

news came as we were sitting down to dine on yet another of the wild chickens that are so plentiful at this time of the year. The farmers call them fool hens because they are so easily caught, although Bertram has yet to get close to one. (The dog brought this one in.) I am so pleased to hear your wonderful news, and although the snow and mud will separate us for only six months of the year, I shall still miss your companionship and conversation. Perhaps we too will have an opportunity to join you. By the way, do you know the difference between a fool hen and my husband? A fool hen will feed a family of four. Your Loving Fanny."

The dwindling population in Larkspur drove the newspapers there into the desperate competition known as the Newspaper Wars. The editor of the *Free Press*'s last remaining competitor, the *Economist*, declared that he "would rather burn in hell than sell to Bell." When it became clear in 1855 that he wouldn't have to travel that far to burn, he made a deal with Homer Bell that merged the two papers into the *Free Press & Economist*, which has published continuously, more or less, ever since.

At the beginning of 1856, Colonel Fortescue was the undisputed business success story of the township, and the Port Petunia *Gleaner* profiled him in its annual special supplement "Ten Men to Watch in Persephone." He was chairman of the Persephone Bank, with branches in Larkspur, Port Petunia, and Demeter Centre, director of the Ontario, Simcoe, and Huron, director of the Port Petunia Harbour Commission, and the man most likely to represent the area in the provincial legislature if the government ever got around to creating a new county out of the rebel townships of Demeter, Pluto, and Persephone. As a businessman, soldier, pioneer, and family man, he was an ideal candidate.

Like so many of the men who have made history, Fortescue now built a monument to remind people of his importance, a many-turreted mansion on Michigan Avenue that he christened Torres Vedras, in homage to one of Wellington's most famous military operations.* Torres Vedras was built on the only rise in Port Petunia, an outcropping of bedrock about fifteen feet high that required water to be carried to it in barrels every day. I have a photograph of that house, but if I were tied up and tortured with a hot poker I still could not tell you what architectural style he had in mind during its construction. The Larkspur *Free Press* had a field day in its assessment of the completed mansion.

> This preposterous pile in Port Petunia combines the Ionic pillars of antiquity with the turrets of a fairy castle and the domes of a Byzantine cathedral. If the reader's taste inclines to the Italianate style, or the Renaissance, or Queen Anne or Greek Revival, he will not feel left out. Several local tradesmen have not been paid for their work, and they have wreaked revenge in a number of ways. The faces of the gargoyles hanging from the door lintels and the cornices bear a striking resemblance to the directors of the Fast Freight railway. The overall effect is that of a circus horse struggling to escape a faux-classical stable.

Fortescue's young wife, Loretta Bakker, daughter of Fritz Bakker, one of the leaders of the Plutonians at the

---

* Wellington was renowned for his prudence in the Peninsular War, retreating quickly in the face of dangerous opposition and husbanding his forces. In this manner he was able to outlast and outwit the French.

Battle of MacNabb's Store, was a pretty farm girl from Pluto Township, fully thirty years his junior, who had been but a slip of a girl when Fortescue led her family to their land grant in the Pluto Marsh. She did not leave the farm again until the day Fortescue came to collect her as a bride in 1838. After producing two sons and a daughter, she was shipped off for a year to a ladies' preparatory school in Toronto, where she was taught to dress and talk like a lady of quality. Fortescue wanted her to move easily in the upper echelons of Port Petunia society, but the experience of finishing school had exactly the opposite effect on poor Loretta, almost finishing her off completely. When she returned to Larkspur, reacquainting herself with her children, she became reclusive and increasingly prone to bouts of nervous prostration, especially when the Colonel was home from one of his wandering business trips. I've heard it said that shortly after the Fortescues completed Torres Vedras, Loretta ordered a piano sent up from Toronto. When the instrument arrived on the Fast Freight, she had the men place it in the front hall. But no sooner had they left than she took an axe and smashed the piano to pieces. The Colonel's next construction project was a special room for Mrs. Fortescue on the third floor of the house's highest tower. She remained there behind barred windows for the next four years.

With the railway completed and his dream of a flourishing port city on Georgian Bay swiftly moving towards realization, Fortescue might have been content to relax and enjoy the fruits of his creation. But as my grandfather points out, this was not in his nature. "As with so many other successful men, the trappings of worldly success did not satisfy the Colonel's restless temperament. He sought new fields to conquer, new peaks to climb. And there was one great enterprise he had long nurtured, a scheme breathtaking in both its scale and its simplicity. So it was that Charles Augustus Fortescue, who had nothing to prove and everything to lose, gambled his reputation and his fortune on a project that had been on his mind ever since he first visited Persephone Township in 1831."

Alert readers will recall that during the original survey of Persephone, Fortescue discovered the shale beach just west of the present site of Port Petunia, now known as Fortescue Beach. For thousands of years the spring ice has ground these rocks as smooth as the bum of a newborn babe and, judging from the diversity of archaeological arti-facts that have collected in the crevices, it has been a popular picnic spot since prehistoric times. While encamped on this long, narrow shelf of flat rock, Fortescue had noted how the shale rocks hissed and spurted streams of blue flame when placed on his campfire. As I mentioned earlier, that evening by their flickering blue light, he wrote feverish notes in his scrapbook and drew the picture of the "Extractor." Much of what he wrote that night is illegible, but we can distinctly make out the phrases "oil distillery" and "petroleum fermentation" in these pages.

The Colonel could see an opportunity for a factory that would provide the town with a steady supply of reasonably priced lamp oil, a substance seldom seen in the early years of the settlement. The pioneers had ample supplies of candle wax for lighting, and their life indoors was chiefly taken up with eating and sleeping. But as Persephone evolved and its residents satisfied their basic needs for shelter and food, they began to look for small luxuries to make their lives more comfortable in the wilderness.

Naturally, being an innovative Canadian entrepreneur with a firm belief in his product, his first stop was the colonial government. He sought out the new premier of the United Province, who was the leader of the old Tory faction, Sir Allan Napier MacNab.* He asked MacNab for government contracts to supply lighting fuel and for help in developing markets beyond Persephone. Premier MacNab enjoyed a speculative flutter and he was impressed with the Colonel's sketches, but he told the aging entrepreneur that he needed some evidence that the process actually worked.

Back in Port Petunia, Fortescue hired a team of local blacksmiths to construct the first prototype of the Steam Extractor, a large boiler that forced steam through a cast-iron chamber that held about a hundred pounds of shale. The kerosene thus sweated from the heated rock dribbled down through a grate and was carried off by brass tubing to a collecting barrel. The Colonel teamed several wagonloads of oil shale from the beach into the railway yards in Port Petunia, where his men had built a smithy. A freight-car-load of cordwood was dumped outside the smithy to heat the boiler.

Naturally the smoke and heat of this enterprise attracted a lot of interest among the townspeople, and a large crowd gathered at the beginning of May 1856 to watch the Extractor go to work on its first load of shale. A reporter from the *Gleaner* was on hand to record the moment.

* Although the spelling of the name is different, the Miller MacNabb and Allan MacNab were undoubtedly cousins. There is a striking physical conformity to this generation of the MacNab-MacNabb clan, and they all left a trail of debts. Allan MacNab claimed to be second in line to the family title, after his older brother Archibald (who used the spelling McNab), who had failed at farming and real estate in Perth, Ontario. Archie McNab is said to have founded the first numbered corporation in the province before leaving the country.

The Colonel and his chief assistant, Mr. Rankin, stood beside their machine attired in leather aprons and top hats, looking every inch the modern equivalent of Vulcan and Mars. They supervised a number of brave young lads stripped to their waists, who shone with sweat as they stoked the boiler and filled the extraction chamber with glistening shale rock. When the gauges registered the required pressure, the Colonel opened the steam release valve with a set of heavy mitts. The Extractor shuddered and rocked, dust and smoke billowed out of the stack, and the alarmed crowd retreated several paces. After an interval, the Colonel walked to the collecting barrel with a pewter mug and turned the small tap.

The citizens waited in expectant silence. When a single drop of clear liquid fell into the mug, it was met with a gasp. The drop was followed by a second and a third, gradually quickening until it turned to a trickle. After fifteen minutes, the Colonel withdrew the mug, poured the contents into a lamp bowl, and struck a match. The wick sputtered, took fire, and blazed into a bright yellow-blue flame. He held the lamp up for all to see. The crowd cheered its enthusiastic approval.

No sooner had the cheer died away, however, than a loud explosion from the Extractor blew out the back wall of the smithy and sent the crowd scrambling up Illinois Street towards the Grand Central Hotel. When the dust cleared and the fire in the railway shed had been damped, it was discovered that an iron plate had blown off the back of the boiler, sheared off a fence post, and embedded itself in the brick wall of the Port Petunia Railway

Station.* Apart from this minor setback, the first test of the Extractor was a dramatic success.

Fortescue had proved that you could squeeze kerosene out of a stone. He would now demonstrate how to extract money from someone else's wallet.

* The restoration of the station has not obscured the iron plate, which is still visible to this day.

Colonel Charles Augustus Fortescue, the "Champlain of Hillhurst County," posed in the uniform of the commanding officer of the Petunia Valley Foot Regiment for this campaign photo taken shortly before the by-election of September 1860.

Chapter 6

THE GREAT OIL SHALE SCANDAL

1856 TO 1866

———◆·◆·◆———

I n my brief time working behind the scenes in politics and
business, I have often been amazed by how the least
promising career can be transformed by a single good
idea. It is equally striking how a brilliant career can be
undone by one mistake.

Dr. Goulding opens his account of Fortescue's march of
folly with a description of the second public trial of the
Steam Extractor.

> The evening of June 14, 1856, provided an unusual
> distraction for the up-and-coming citizens of Port
> Petunia. For this was the occasion on which the Tory
> prime minister of the Canadas, one of the founders of
> the new-minted Liberal-Conservative Party, Sir Allan
> Napier MacNab, came to Persephone. The affable
> premier had served with "conspicuous gallantry" in
> the War of 1812 and had been knighted for his quick
> action with the Toronto militia to suppress the 1837

rebellion.* A lucrative law practice plus numerous speculations in land and business had given him access to huge lines of credit which he diverted into railways, shipping, and the construction of Dundurn Castle, his magnificent residence in Hamilton, which made Fortescue's Torres Vedras look like a cottage. By the time he arrived in Port Petunia, MacNab was hopelessly extended and teetering on the edge of financial ruin. But he was greeted like a visiting Duke of Wellington.

It was quite a junket, according to the Port Petunia *Gleaner*. MacNab brought along his commissioner responsible for public works and his friend the ever-observant Judge Ridout, plus their personal secretaries, two special assistants, and a transportation consultant. The express reason for their visit was "to see Colonel Fortescue's rebuilt Oil Shale Extractor put to a trial."

Imagine the scene. As the train pulled in, well-dressed citizens crowded the Port Petunia station and the Petunia Valley Foot regimental brass band struck up a stirring rendition of "God Save the Queen." The premier stepped off the train onto a raised dais, where he was welcomed by Colonel Fortescue, resplendent in the uniform of a major general of the Petunia Valley Foot Regiment. His elder son, Reginald, now assistant general manager of the Persephone Bank, stood beside him. In the light of burning torches, Fortescue gave a short welcoming speech that was cheered lustily by the crowd. Then MacNab and his party were

---

* Ms. Cameron has pointed out that MacNab also served in the same regiment as Fortescue when he was still a camp cook. She feels strongly that the premier and Fortescue knew each other and, more important, that the wily politician had Fortescue's number.

transported to the south end of Michigan Avenue, where they were installed in guest rooms in the east wing of Torres Vedras. (It was not as susceptible to the Westerlies that so often howled in from the bay.)

Judge Ridout mentions that Mrs. Fortescue did not attend the banquet in MacNab's honour that evening. Fortescue gave her regrets, saying that she was suffering from "the summer complaint."

The next morning, Premier MacNab spoke to the crowd from the balcony of Torres Vedras. He told them how impressed he was with the "energy and enthusiasm of the people of Persephone" and expressed confidence that "Port Petunia has great days ahead of it." When a voice challenged him from the crowd, demanding his policies, he replied: "All my politics are Railroad!"

The *Gleaner* resumes the story.

After lunch, the official party drove down Michigan Avenue to the rail yards for the second trial of the Extractor, which had been hauled out to the shoreline and surrounded by a high wall of sandbags. The employees of the nearby train station had taken the precaution of protecting the windows with feather mattresses and had suspended access by passengers until the trial was over. The Premier and his colleagues donned leather aprons, iron helmets, and face shields. Fortescue drew his sabre, pointed it to the sky, and shouted, "By the miracles of modern scientific discovery, we lead ourselves out of darkness and into light. Let the trial begin!"

As it had on the first test, the Extractor shuddered and belched great quantities of smoke and ash. After the gauges reached the pressure levels required for extraction, Fortescue strode towards the steam release valve and opened it using a twelve-foot cedar pole. As before, a trickle of kerosene soon emerged from the collection barrel and the Colonel gathered the liquid in his pewter mug. He charged the lamp bowl, struck a match to the wick, and was rewarded with a bright flame. The premier beamed and shook hands with the entrepreneur. The crowd applauded briefly, then turned and jogged down the street to a safe distance. But this time, the boiler held, and the official party returned to the bar in the Grand Central Hotel for a serious discussion about the future. When they emerged late that afternoon, Fortescue had assurances of the highest level of support, and the premier himself had agreed to serve as a director for the new Persephone Oil Shale Company.

These were optimistic days in the province as well as in Persephone. My grandfather describes how the government-financed railway boom of the 1850s created unbridled speculation in the Canadas. From Port Petunia the fever spread quickly to the surrounding townships: "As with most economic booms, good times were fuelled by great expectations rather than by any underlying increase in productivity. Workers emptied out of the mills and stores to join the stampede to the gold fields of California and Australia. This drove wage rates higher and caused the good farmers of the Pine River plains to pause at their plows and scratch their heads, wondering if they were in the right occupation. Why should they ruin their health in the fields for pennies when they could speculate in railway shares for pounds?"

A few days after MacNab's visit, Colonel Fortescue announced the formation of the Persephone Oil Shale Company, 1856. The following Saturday night, residents flocked to the Port Petunia Town Hall to hear the Colonel address a public meeting called to explain his company's prospectus and solicit investors. Standing in front of a set of easels holding financial charts, he claimed that the Oil Shale Company would produce one thousand barrels of kerosene a month. At a market price of 50 cents a gallon, this would give the company gross monthly revenues of $17,500 by the end of the year. As he held the only proven source of kerosene in the province, and given the estimated size of the deposit, Fortescue foresaw breathtaking possibilities for his enterprise. The initial public offering of stock was pegged at $1 per share, which the Colonel confidently predicted would double as soon as the plant reached full production. "You need only cast your bread out upon the waters," he urged the crowd.

As the applause died down, the *Gleaner* reports, a voice called out: "Keep yoor money in yoor troosers! Cast yoor bread out upon the waters and it will coom back to you as soggy bread!" There is no mistaking the voice of Big Sandy MacKelvey, who must have ridden in from Larkspur with his supporters. But there is no evidence his warning had any effect. Except for the bitter burghers of Larkspur, everyone in the county jumped at the chance to get in on the next big thing, as Dr. Goulding describes.

> Men and women emptied their savings accounts and rummaged through mattresses in a fever of speculative frenzy. Allan MacNab put himself down for a hundred shares and touted the stock among his friends in the city. The first share offering sold out within two weeks, bringing in subscribers from Toronto to Montreal. The second offering, at $5, and the third, at $10, both sold smartly. By the beginning of July 1856, the enterpris-

ing Colonel had a capital base of $200,000, a sum roughly nine times the total tax base of the Township. That winter, Persephonites huddled around their stoves with visions of riches dancing in their heads. The following spring, farmers left their fields fallow and turned livestock out on the pastures to fend for itself as virtually every able-bodied man, woman, and child over the age of twelve in the community plunged into the task of building the factory.

Perhaps never before or since has the stony face of Pipesmoke Mountain looked down on such feverish activity in Persephone. On a plateau about three hundred yards south of the shale beach, Fortescue marked out the foundations and started spending the shareholders' money. The timberlands of the Petunia River echoed to the sound of axes, and Port Petunia's four sawmills worked second shifts to produce square beams and straight boards. The Larkspur Distillery worked around the clock to handle the increased demand. An engineering crew arrived from the city to supervise the construction.

By the fall of 1857, a building two hundred feet long and sixty feet wide that could accommodate four giant versions of the Extractor had risen from the foundations. A separate machine shop was built, and masons went to work on two massive stone chimneys to carry away the smoke and fumes produced by the extraction process. The sound of sledgehammers ricocheted off the ever-steeper walls of the oil shale quarries, and pumps worked day and night to return the seeping lake water to the bay. Beer flowed freely in the hotels on Michigan Avenue. By November, the first Extractor was in operation, with a hundred men employed to feed wood and rock into it and seventy-five more to work in the quarries. The chimneys belched a plume that was visible to the citizens of Toronto. Little did they know what was going up with that smoke.

The climate in Persephone has a nasty habit of spoiling the best-laid plans. Winter struck hard that year, bringing operations to a complete halt in the first week of January 1858, but spirits in the community remained high. The share price of the Persephone Oil Shale Company had climbed to $50. The Colonel took delivery of a second piano for his parlour on the main floor, and an artist arrived to paint his likeness, which now hangs in the Station House Museum. Loretta Fortescue did not sit with her husband for the portrait, and nothing is known about the state of her mental health at this time.

In the spring of 1858, the Extractor went back into operation, now producing about three barrels of kerosene a week. Few people noticed that this plateau was reached a year late and was much lower than predicted in the original prospectus. Even fewer had the temerity to question the Colonel on such a small point, for "every great enterprise must go through its growth pains," as my grandfather put it.

Something else arrived in Port Petunia that summer via the Fast Freight, "news that fell on the community like the ominous tinkling of the chandeliers over the Grand Staircase of the Titanic as it bumped gently against an iceberg in the North Atlantic," Dr. Goulding would write. "A travelling salesman propping up the bar at the Grand Central Hotel, after a long day of hawking a restorative hair tonic, remarked that he'd enjoyed particularly good business in Lambton County the month before. It seemed a local farmer had discovered a deposit of black oil on his property, and a group of entrepreneurs were investigating ways of removing the oil by means of deep wells.* He observed that the speculative boom in Lambton was very much like the fever which now gripped Persephone."

Unfazed, Colonel Fortescue moved quickly to counteract the negative publicity. As a student of the art of public relations, I must give the Colonel credit for his instinctive grasp of what we now call "the three Ds" of damage control: defend, deny, and distract. In September he printed up tracts and distributed them to his investors, insisting on the purity of Persephone kerosene and warning buyers not to be fooled by cheap imitations. He pointed out that so far no one had actually drilled a producing well in Lambton County and that the product was "filthy, sulphurous, and foul-smelling" while Persephone's was "light, amber, and sweet, like the finest Larkspur whisky." This was patently untrue, as anyone who has ever tasted Larkspur's distillations will tell you.

By the end of 1858, the sum total of production at the Persephone Oil Shale Works reached one hundred barrels a month, far less than the originally projected one thousand. Work had not even started on the second Extractor and, at current market rates, the total inventory of the

---

* "Discovered" is probably not the most accurate word to use in this case. Farmers do not discover things in the same way that a Champlain or a Frobisher does. The farmer "noticed" one day that all his cows were lying dead out in the field, and he mentioned this at breakfast with his wife. While dragging the carcasses downwind, he reflected on the proximity of the dead cows to the pool of oil. This was the precise point when he realized that an economic opportunity had presented itself. Then, being a typically resourceful and enterprising Ontario farmer, he jumped on the buckboard, drove into town, and sued the township for the value of his cows.

company on hand would have scarcely covered Sir Allan's own personal investment in the scheme. But Fortescue's vigorous promotional efforts kept the share price firm. When an editorial in the upstart *Northern Intelligence* newspaper in Port Petunia dared to suggest that the first Extractor spent as much time under repair as producing kerosene, the Colonel responded with a libel suit that drove it out of business.

With the winter shutdown in early 1859, the rumours subsided, but in the spring we find the Colonel appearing before Port Petunia Town Council to defend the Persephone Oil Shale Company and insist that its product was selling well in "foreign markets."* "The inferior grade of crude oil being distilled in Southwestern Ontario will never be able to compete with Persephone's nectar," he said. But there was little the Colonel could do about the two short items that appeared a few days later on the back page of the *Gleaner*. The first reported that wells near Oil Springs, Ontario, had been drilled deep enough to produce crude oil that was sufficiently sludge-free to run freely through a pipe. (The Extractor had never produced enough kerosene to run through much more than a straw.) The second item noted that the market price of kerosene had slipped from 50 cents a gallon to 30 cents.

Incredibly, nothing happened. Production at the factory continued and the share price held over the summer, as the price of kerosene slowly dropped to 20 cents and then 15, just above the cost of production advertised in the Oil Shale Company prospectus. "A temporary adjustment," insisted Fortescue in an interview with the *Gleaner*. "The fundamentals of the market are strong."

---

* One barrel of kerosene had been sold in Buffalo.

Then, in July of 1859, the *Gleaner* printed an anonymous letter to the editor from a disgruntled former employee of the Persephone Bank, claiming that this august institution was dangerously overextended in loans to the Oil Shale Company.

Some readers may find the above scenario painfully similar to recent unpleasantnesses in the markets. Those investors who got skinned by mutual funds in the 1970s – or government bonds in the 1980s or real estate in the 1990s or tech stocks in the 2000s – hardly need a scolding voice from 1859 to ask, "What were you thinking?" Sensitive readers might well choose to skip on to the next chapter. But I feel it is important to demonstrate that the Michael Bliss paradigm has been hard at work in this country for at least 150 years.

In late September, Fortescue issued a "profit warning," advising investors that "the recent decline in kerosene prices may have ushered in a new world order of slower growth for the home illumination industry." However, he foresaw only a short period of soft prices before the market rebounded and described the present downturn as "a strong buying opportunity" for the company's shares. As for the Persephone Bank, he said that there was "no need to panic."

This was a mistake. Nothing starts a run on the bank faster than a man in a suit telling people not to be alarmed. On a Monday morning in late September, farmers rushed into Port Petunia to stand in line at the doors of the bank. In the boardroom inside, Fortescue held an emergency meeting with his directors.

The Colonel finally made an appearance on the front steps of the bank building and delivered a speech about the solid assets of the bank, the bright future ahead for clean-burning kerosene, and the steadily improving state of the farm economy. He promised on his honour as "a British officer, a veteran of the War of 1812, and a loyal Persephonite" that each of his depositors would be paid in hard coin. (It's hard to know where such coin might have come from.) If people stood with him now, the bank would survive, he promised, which gave them a greater chance of recovering their deposits. Moreover, and this was the cleverest ploy, the bank would not have to call in its loans. The Colonel knew perfectly well that practically every depositor had a relative on the farm with a mortgage held by the bank. After a good deal of grumbling, the crowd dispersed and went home.

You have to hand it to Fortescue. He had defended and denied with considerable skill, putting his foot wrong only once with the P-word. He now moved on to distract the citizens of Persephone with a public relations coup that I would happily have added to my own resumé. During the dreary month of November 1859, joyful headlines appeared in the two remaining township newspapers, the Port Petunia *Gleaner* and the Larkspur *Free Press & Economist*. "Prince of Wales Promises Visit to Port Petunia!" "H.R.H. to Make Pilgrimage to Persephone!" screamed the headlines. Colonel Charles Augustus Fortescue had been in contact with the organizers of the Royal Tour of the Canadas scheduled for the summer of 1860. And to his great delight, he was pleased to announce that Port Petunia was on the itinerary. With a single stroke, Fortescue had distracted the attention of the community from his financial troubles and provided himself with the perfect launching pad for his final quest: political office.

All worries about the future of the Oil Shale Company and the Persephone Bank vanished in the heat of patriotic fervour that enveloped the township as it threw itself into preparations for the Prince's visit, which would conveniently occur only one week before a by-election for the new riding of Hillhurst. (The government had finally decided to group some of the rebel townships together; Demeter, Pluto, and Persephone now formed Hillhurst County.) A few weeks after the Royal Tour was announced, Fortescue declared his candidacy for the seat under the banner of the Liberal-Conservatives. His main support would come from the boom town of Port Petunia.

Just to be sure Fortescue had some opposition, Big Sandy MacKelvey threw his hat in the ring as an independent. But his political base wasn't nearly as robust. Larkspur's population had by now dwindled to fewer than five hundred people, and it had lost its status as the political capital of the township. The voters would now have to make the trip into Port Petunia on election day. Big Sandy could summon up the support of the citizens of Larkspur and many of the farmers in the drumlins, but he couldn't fight the one-two punch of the Prince and Progress.

The Port Petunia Town Council appointed a committee to take charge of the royal visit and chose as its chairperson Mrs. Archibald Smart, founder of the Terpsichore Society and one of the leading cultural lights of the town. Adelaide seized the reins and installed her sister, Fanny, on the executive.

Politics and planning combined to heat the rivalry between the two towns to new levels of nastiness. In the spring of 1860 the Algonquin Railway finally reached Larkspur and headed down the Pine River to Port Petunia. It was due to go into service just a few weeks before the Prince's visit. Big Sandy's supporters agitated for the Prince to arrive on the Hog Special through the drumlins by way of Larkspur, which would allow him to visit both

towns. Fortescue's forces derailed that idea by blocking
the route of the Hog Special as the construction crew
approached Port Petunia, forcing a delay that was fatal to
Larkspur's bid for the Royal Tour.

As the great day approached, the citizens of Port
Petunia could barely contain their excitement. Adelaide had
gone overboard with her plans for the decorations. The
royal guests would travel from the station in an open carriage drawn by six white horses, passing under no fewer
than ten massive triumphal arches of spruce boughs (fes-
tooned with garlands of maple leaves painted crimson to
simulate their fall colours) on their way to the steamer *Mary
Anne* for a pleasant afternoon cruise on Georgian Bay. She
purchased miles of bunting and commissioned the production of a thousand Chinese lanterns for the street decorations. She assembled the regimental brass band and taught
them to play "The Prince Consort March," which effectively
doubled their repertoire. Members of the Terpsichore
Society dressed as Huron warriors would run beside the
Prince's coach. Adelaide insisted on a twenty-one-gun can-
nonade, even though the town owned only one real cannon
and it had not been fired since being captured from the
Russians in the Crimea five years before. The rest would be
wooden replicas made out of fence posts painted black.
Archie, the local munitions expert, was appointed to see to
their "firing." Schoolchildren of the district would be
dressed up as obscure characters of Greek myth. As a final
touch, Adelaide had persuaded the mayor and the members
of Port Petunia Town Council to appear as Poseidon and his
sea courtiers and to station themselves on the jetty beside
the *Mary Anne*.

Several days before the visit, idle workers from the Oil
Shale Works erected a large podium at the foot of Michigan

Avenue beside the harbourmaster's office and decorated it with bunting, flags, spruce trees, pumpkins, cornstalks, and wheat sheaves. Adelaide then wrote the script for a pageant to be enacted for the Prince, a fascinating work of which one copy survives.* The work had to be cut down from the original, which is said to have run slightly longer than Wagner's Ring Cycle and could not have been performed in its entirety without overnight accommodation for the audience and reinforcement for the stage. She also put her son, George Gordon Smart, to work on a narrative poem to be read to the Prince. He chose a suitably epic subject that had much to say about the history of the township: "The Twenty-Nine Close Calls of the *Mary Anne*."

George Gordon was a vague and dreamy sort who spent a good part of his time sitting in graveyards and wrote verses about shipwrecks, train wrecks, runaway teams, floods, and grass fires, almost always involving great loss of life and a good deal of property damage. His latest work was inspired by a recent event that he knew would strike close to the hearts of several people on the platform, above all the future prime minister of Canada, John A. Macdonald.

My vigilant associate, Ms. Cameron, uncovered a news-paper clipping from the *Gleaner* from the fall of 1859 reporting a little-known incident on Georgian Bay that holds some significance for the events that were about to unfold. A large party of prominent citizens that included Macdonald, then attorney general of Canada West, had passed through Port Petunia, taking ship on the *Ploughboy*, a paddlewheel steamboat with many near misses in its career.

* In the archives of the Terpsichore Society, which are fiercely protected by the great-granddaughter of Adelaide, Ms. Phoebe Fitz.

While negotiating the tricky outward passage between Hawk Island and the Hatchling Islands, in rough seas, the steamboat's steering gear failed, and she drifted helplessly towards the precipitous cliffs of Hawk Island. With a heavy swell of the sea setting towards the shore and a gale blowing directly upon the breakers, imminent death faced every man, woman, and child on board. Husbands and wives all said a last poignant farewell, dropped to their knees in prayer, and commended themselves to Providence. But at a distance of only forty-five yards from land, the anchors that had been set out for the last five miles finally caught bottom and held the ship fast. She remained in this position from sundown on that evening until noon the next day, when the water calmed enough for the crew to ferry the passengers ashore in a small boat and raise the alarm. Huddled that night beside an open fire on the beach, Macdonald is said to have remarked that it would be a frosty day in the tropics before he ever set foot on another "iron barge out of Port Petunia." Soon a rescue vessel from the port rushed to the steamer's assistance, towing her to safety with no loss of life and only a modest repair contract in the Petunia Shipyard. This near-death experience had a profound effect on Macdonald. He was never again comfortable at sea and always had to fortify himself with a quantity of gin before he could be persuaded to venture across rough water – or a damp street. Ms. Cameron tells me that the steamer reappeared on the lakes the next season rechristened the *Mary Anne*.

The visit of the Prince of Wales came at a crucial time for British North America. The British government, tired of mouldy Canadian wheat, wormy Canadian apples, and endless barrels of rancid Canadian butter, began to look at different strategies for getting rid of its North American colonies without making their expulsion look deliberate. Naturally, colonial leaders were reluctant to sever ties with the mother country because they were all counting on a knighthood and a posting to Bermuda in their old age. But the new colonial secretary, Henry Pelham, Duke of Newcastle, knew that sending the randy young prince unchaperoned to Canada was bound to produce a groundswell of support for a confederation of the provinces, an idea floated originally by the Reform Party some years before.*

On Sunday, August 12, 1860, the month-long Royal Tour of the Canadas commenced when the British naval vessel *Hero* and her little escort of ships sailed into Gaspé Harbour, the first stop of its stately progress up the St. Lawrence River. Wherever the Royal Tour touched land, it was greeted with an outpouring of patriotic fervour, a passion that was returned in different kind by the young prince. Albert Edward, or Bertie, as his family called him, was clearly delighted to be off on his own, away from the strictures of court life under his prudish mother, Queen Victoria, and his moralizing father, Prince Albert. Bertie was only a year away from his first scandal at military school and already showing a precocious interest in "actresses," champagne, and horses.

This was the first visit by a crown prince of England to the colonies in living memory. It had been nearly seventy-five years since his great-uncle the Duke of Clarence (later William IV) had cut an erotic swath across the colonies of British North America and left an uncounted number of North American pretenders to the throne of England. Bertie

---

* The Reform Party of Ontario and Quebec in the mid-nineteenth century should not be confused with the late-twentieth-century Reform Party, which believed Ottawa should plant tulips every spring and paint the Peace Bridge once in a while but attempt nothing else.

had no doubt read his great-uncle's report that the colonies were "a very gay and lively place full of women, and those of the most obliging kind."* Once again the society matrons of the Canadas made ready to unlock their daughters.

The Prince paused at Quebec City to hand out honours in the Legislative Assembly, at Montreal to open the Victoria Bridge, and at Ottawa to lay the cornerstone of the new Parliament Buildings. He continued by steamboat, canoe, carriage, and rail to Brockville on Lake Ontario, then on to Kingston, where he ran into the first protest demonstration of the trip. Members of the Orange Lodge, forbidden to display their insignia in public in Britain, for fear of inciting violence among the Irish, refused to put away their banners. The Prince's guardian, the Duke of Newcastle, warned that it would create problems at home if the Prince appeared to endorse the lodge in any way. The royal steamer sat offshore overnight, waiting for the Orangemen to disband. When they were still there in the morning, the steamer moved on, leaving the townspeople of Kingston crestfallen. Macdonald stayed behind to comfort his constituents, but he caught up to the tour in Toronto just as it set out for Persephone.

The day of the royal visit to Port Petunia, September 10, 1860, dawned sunny and bright. A convivial regal party climbed into the special car laid on by the board of directors of the OSHUR (renamed the Ontario, Simcoe, and Huron Union Railway just before the Royal Tour, to protect the innocent) and steamed north in a haze of cigar smoke and champagne bubbles. The royal party included the governor general, Sir Edmund Walker Head, and John

* Anne Somerset, *The Life and Times of William IV* (Weidenfeld and Nicolson, 1993), p. 46.

A. Macdonald, who was by now sharing the leadership of the Canadas with his colleague George-Étienne Cartier, co-leader of the Liberal-Conservative Party.*

At the station in Port Petunia, "a surging crowd of fifteen thousand people waited in a state of high expectation," according to the *Gleaner*. Larkspur's newspapers put the number at closer to fifteen hundred. Whatever its size, the young man clad in "a tasteful grey suit of Canadian design" took one look at the assemblage and paled visibly. The Prince had by now endured thirty such receptions, all involving cannons, triumphal arches, levee, lunch, ball, pageant, recitation, dinner, fireworks, and brass bands. He straightened his shoulders and walked forward with the grim resignation of a man being handed over to torture and the gallows. When John A. saw his old nemesis the *Ploughboy* tied up at the wharf, "he shied like a horse meeting its first locomotive and disappeared into the saloon of the Grand Central Hotel, stumbling over his ceremonial sword in his haste," the *Gleaner* continued. She might have been rechristened the *Mary Anne*, but John A. knew her instantly.

Noticeably absent from the party on the reviewing stand was the general manager of the Persephone Bank, Reginald Fortescue, the Colonel's older son. The Colonel explained that young Reggie was "on business south of the

* Whether Macdonald called himself Conservative or Liberal depended on which province he was speaking from. He was Conservative in Ontario and Liberal in Quebec. The reader is encouraged not to make too much of the official names of Canadian political parties in the nineteenth century. The rule of thumb is that all parties tend to behave like Liberals during an election, but they become Conservative when they form a government. When they lose an election very badly, they retreat to third-party status and call for reform, separation, and the building of another railway. If a Conservative loses a rural election, he is sent to bed without supper.

border," but it struck some as odd that the main financial institution in the community would go unrepresented at the social event of the century.

I've pieced together the dramatic account that follows from many sources assembled by Ms. Cameron, among them the two newspapers, Fanny's diary, and the records of the Terpsichore Society. I welcome any additional information readers can provide about what really happened on this famous day.

Archie Smart ordered the salute. As the Prince approached the platform with the governor general, twenty wooden cannons exploded on the breakwall in a shower of kindling and small stones, sending the platform party diving off their chairs onto the carpet in fear of assassination. When the commotion died down, Fortescue stepped forward in the striking scarlet and gold regalia of the commanding officer of the Petunia Valley Foot Regiment. Weighted down by his campaign medals, gold epaulettes, and sword, he looked much the way a heavily decorated doorman at the Royal York Hotel in Toronto looks today. Perhaps because of his failing eyesight, he mistook the young man in the grey Canadian tweed suit for a bodyguard. Turning his back on the royal guest, he proceeded to read out the town's address to the governor general, who was easier to spot since he was wearing a scarlet uniform and plumed cockade hat. After a few minutes of this, Sir Edmund turned Fortescue firmly around by the shoulders to face his future sovereign and said, "There's the man you're looking for, old stick. Carry on."

The speeches droned on, much in the way they do for civic events under the town clock of Port Petunia today. Before long the wind shifted, bringing a blast of arctic air in off the bay. The temperature dropped 30 degrees, ominous black clouds formed in the northwest, and whitecaps danced on the grey-green waters of the harbour. As George Gordon Smart rose to declaim the opening verse of his sixty-three-stanza poem, the first of the triumphal arches blew over.

"'Twas a stormy day on Georgian Bay, when the *Mary Anne* set sail," he shouted.

> With four and fifty passengers hanging off the rail.
> Old Captain Price stood at the helm, his pipe
>   clenched in his mouth,
> And noted how the wind was up and backed into the
>   south . . .

The governor general blinked his eyes once in disbelief like a bemused fruit bat and tilted his cocked hat down over his nose.

> She was bound for Manitoulin with a load of bricks
>   and flour,
> One Shorthorn cow and twenty ducks and coal for
>   extra power.
> The first mate scanned the western sky. "Oh,
>   Captain," he did say.
> "I fear the sight of yon high cloud – a gale is on its
>   way."

> But the captain laughed and smacked his pipe against
>   the smoking stack.
> "I fear no breeze that comes my way, we sure ain't
>   turnin' back."

The Prince of Wales stood up suddenly and said, "Jolly good, thank you. Time for a sail, what?" The royal party dutifully trotted after him down the steps and over to the jetty, where Poseidon and his finned acolytes were waiting to hand them up the gangway to the *Mary Anne*. The little ship rocked violently against her ropes, but the Prince leapt aboard with a grin. Someone ran to the Grand Central to fetch Macdonald, who had to be supported up the gangway by two officers of the royal bodyguard. No sooner had the crew cast off than another blast from the channel between Hawk Island and the Hatchlings bore down on the crowd huddled on the wharf, sending several hats into the water and bowling over two more of the spruce arches. The ship heeled over to starboard, bringing the port paddlewheel clear of the water. The sound of smashing crockery could be heard.

"D'ye think the lad is safe?" asked one of the councillors.

"Never fear," said Arthur Dodd, the old harbourmaster, "the *Mary Anne* has come through worse than this."

Back at the podium, George Gordon was still in full poetical flight, unaware that the object of his recitation had fled. His adoring mother, Adelaide, watched raptly from the platform stairs.

> It would have filled their hearts with dread to think a
> > day from now,
> The only soul left on that ship would be that
> > Shorthorn cow . . .

Suddenly a cry went up from the crowd at the pier. Arms pointed to the north. A massive bank of sea fog had appeared at the entrance to the harbour and was now rolling towards the *Mary Anne* with astonishing speed.

"Stand by the salvage boats!" shouted Dodd. "Sound the fog bells! All men to the boats!"

The fog bank swallowed up the bobbing *Mary Anne*. Women screamed. The wind dropped suddenly, but the waves continued to crash against the jetty.

"She'll hit the breakwall for sure!"

"Mark the position," shouted Harbourmaster Dodd. "Pay out the lines and make for her at all speed."

Say what you like about the Port Petunia Shipyard workers, in an emergency they know their work. Dodd jumped into the rescue skiff and stood in the bow while eight stout men rowed with all their might to the spot where the *Mary Anne* had last been seen. Two lines leading from huge winches on the wharf rattled out of their drums, following the wake of the skiff. Before long, the rescuers melted into the fog, and all that could be seen was the trailing lines. Alone on the podium and now lost in a fog himself, George Gordon continued his oration.

The dreadful waves ride higher still, o'er each she
    tries to ride,
There was an awful ripping sound and then – the
    engines died.
"Oh, Captain, we must lose some freight," the fearful
    mate implored.
The Captain snarled, "Bring up the ducks and throw
    them overboard."

After an agonizing wait that couldn't have been more than ten minutes but seemed like hours to the crowd, there was a crash and shouts in the distance.

"Haul away!" came the distant cry.

The great winches on the jetty turned, the lines lifted out of the water, and all held their breath, straining to make out a shape in the dense fog.

"It's her!" cried Archie Smart. "She's saved again!"

The *Mary Anne* loomed out of the mist, bravely bobbing on the choppy waves. Harbourmaster Dodd stood at the wheelhouse door with Captain Price and the Prince. Bertie waved jauntily and the crowd cheered, then gasped. There was a thirty-foot gash down the starboard side, and the paddlewheel was crushed from its contact with the break-wall, but the bilge pumps were somehow keeping the doughty steamer afloat. The winches brought her up against the wharf, but not without another grinding crash that broke more wineglasses topside.

As the wind rose and the fog lifted, the Prince trotted down the gangway to great applause and handshakes. The governor general followed, holding a handkerchief to a nasty cut on his forehead. John A. was carried out on a door and delivered by carriage back to the waiting train.

On the lonely reviewing stand, the frayed bunting flapped around the Bard of Persephone as he shouted the closing stanzas of his epic into the teeth of a rising gale.

> And then they saw the breakers pound upon the
>   distant shore,
> The first mate sobbed, "Oh, Captain, sir! We stand at
>   Heaven's door!"
> But the Captain turned her broadside and steered
>   with just one hand.
> "I think there's still a chance," he grinned. "That
>   beach ahead is sand."
>
> She ran aground in softest muck, as gently as a babe
> Is wrapped in flannel blankets and in a cradle laid.
> The passengers stepped off and vowed next time
>   they'd take the train,

But Old Captain Price walked home that night and
> he lived to sail again.

On the station platform, Fortescue mumbled his apologies to the Prince for the confusion.

"No damage," said the Prince. "Always keep a stern line out, I say. Sorry we can't stay for tea." Then he turned to Sir Edmund and said, "Great-Uncle Willy was right, Stinky. None of us come here for our health.* I promise you'll get Bermuda before the year is out."† He then turned to his guardian and said, "We've done our bit, Henry. Do you think maybe we could do Paris next summer?"

The Royal Tour of 1860 far exceeded the colonial secretary's wildest hopes. As soon as the Prince returned home, he told the horrified queen about the conditions in Canada. Nine months later, letters were streaming in from Canadian mothers, each claiming to have produced a new heir to the throne. This threw Prince Albert into a fit of apoplexy that weakened his constitution sufficiently for the typhoid to carry him off in 1861. Queen Victoria went into seclusion, ostensibly in mourning for her husband, but some say she vowed privately not to appear again in public until Canada achieved its independence. She was almost true to her word. One of her first public appearances after Albert's death was at the opening of Parliament in February 1867, just a week before the introduction of the British North America Act, which paved the way for the confederation of the Canadian

---

* This remark is commonly attributed to Prince Philip, on a Canadian tour in the 1980s. In fact, the words were first spoken on the first royal visit in 1786, by the future William IV, and have been repeated by every royal visitor since.

† Actually, he got to be governor of the Hudson's Bay Company back in London, which was even better.

provinces. Not until the year of Queen Victoria's death did a future king set foot on Canadian soil again.

The Latin inscription on the bronze plaque placed on the Port Petunia jetty by the Terpsichore Society to mark the abrupt end of the Royal Tour of 1860 is still visible, although weathered by wind and spray: "Arma Principemque cano . . . I sing of arms and the Prince, who first from the shores of England braved shipwreck and privation to lift the hearts of his subjects in the Canadas. God Save the Queen."

Colonel Fortescue rode a wave of patriotic euphoria through the final week of the by-election campaign. No one seemed to think it strange that he had declared an extended "Bank Holiday to Celebrate the Royal Visit." This kept the Oil Shale Works and the Persephone Bank closed until after the voting. Against this juggernaut, Big Sandy was reduced to desperate measures. On election day, September 17, he deployed the most effective political weapon at his disposal: the Larkspur Distillery. To each of his poll captains he issued a barrel of rye whisky, and he escorted them to various posts around the Port Petunia Town Hall to intercept voters arriving from the outposts of the township.

Elections were rough-and-tumble affairs in those days, with the secret ballot still ten years off. Intimidation of the voters was considered an essential element of the overall campaign. The eminent historian D.G. Creighton could have been describing the 1860 Hillhurst by-election when he wrote: "These were the days of the open poll, when each vote was a blow which was known and cheered, and when the electors on both sides marched to the hustings like the men-at-arms of two medieval private armies."*

* Donald Creighton, *John A. Macdonald: The Young Politician* (Macmillan, 1952), p. 98.

When the poll opened at ten o'clock in the morning, the brisk wind carried the promise of snow. Colonel Fortescue rode from Torres Vedras down Michigan Avenue to the town hall on a white horse, followed by scores of workers from the factory and the shale quarries. A huge crowd milled around the town hall, where Big Sandy had already taken up his position with a number of his kinsmen from Larkspur and the surrounding highlands. As the returning officer read out a name from the voters' list, one of Big Sandy's supporters would shout a vote in favour of his chief. Any man who tried to speak up for Fortescue received a smart crack on the jaw. Fortescue's men charged the steps and were flung back down. Men rolled in the mud, dogs barked, the people cheered, and little boys ran through the crowd selling hot chestnuts.

Late that morning, with the arrival of the Petunia Valley Foot, the tide turned in favour of Fortescue. The boisterous proceedings went on until dark, when the tally was announced as 475 for the Colonel and 227 for Big Sandy. The returning officer formally posed the question of Big Sandy whether he wished to retire and concede the contest to Fortescue.

Dr. Goulding relates the events that followed the announcement of the voting.

Big Sandy had just opened his mouth to speak when a man galloped up Michigan Avenue on a horse.

"Reginald Fortescue has been arrested at the border," he shouted. "He is being held by the Americans for his father's debts!"

"It must be a misunderstanding," exclaimed the Colonel. "They have no right – "

"'Tis true. The price of kerosene has dropped to one cent a gallon and they say the oil stocks are worthless!"

In the flickering torchlight, with no money in their pockets and the first snow of an approaching winter swirling in the air, the citizens of Persephone sobered up very quickly.

"What did ah tell yoo!" yelled Big Sandy. "There he is! The man who gave us riches from rocks! He said he would make grass grow in Larkspur's streets. He'll nae rest until Port Petunia looks the same!"

"Down with the liar Fortescue!" cried the crowd. "To the bank!"

The angry mob surged forward as one, all party faction dissolved by their anger. They dragged the Colonel from his horse and bundled him into a wagon, which led the march down Michigan Avenue to the Persephone Bank building. When the door to the bank would not yield, the men smashed the windows and climbed inside. They pried the combination to the safe out of the Colonel and swung open the great door . . . to find the vault was empty save for neat rows of folders holding the mortgages of the farmers and merchants of the township.

There was no stopping the mob now. Fortescue was trussed to a rail and carried to the edge of town, where the doors of the Oil Shale Works yielded to the assault. Inside they stoked up the Steam Extractor until the fires reached their peak and the furnaces glowed red with the heat. Then they dumped Fortescue into the ore chamber and slammed the big iron door shut. In spite of the roar of the crowd and the rumblings of the infernal machine, Fortescue's terrible shrieks could be heard above it all.

The inquest ordered by the provincial government into the circumstances of his death found that Fortescue had been the victim of an "unfortunate industrial accident" and recommended that a steel grate be installed on all future Extractors to prevent a similar occurrence. His remains were consigned to a cigar box and left on the front doorstep of Torres Vedras. Big Sandy was elected the member for Hillhurst by acclamation. The farmers returned to their neglected homesteads to report to their wives and children that their savings were gone. So began the Winter of the Turnip, when the population tightened their belts and returned to the staple diet that had seen them through the first hard years of settlement. It was all very difficult for the older people to accept after twenty-five years of back-breaking labour.

The only resident whose life seems to have been unaffected by the collapse of the township economy was Fanny Haddock. Her Christmas card to Adelaide that year reported: "Castor, Pollux, and Calliope are working at the lumber camps in Euthanasia Township. (Calliope is quite the inventive cook!) There is more snow than usual and the neighbourhood boys are catching me lots of rabbits. I am well and there is no other news to report. Affectionately, Fanny."

The doors and windows of the Persephone Bank were boarded up. No smoke issued from the chimneys of the Oil Shale Works. The citizens made it through the winter thanks to a load of rice sent out by the government as a relief gesture, the first welfare payment to the township since 1834. Over the next few months, the residents ransacked the factory and carried away every stick of timber and iron fitting for use on their farms.

By the fall of 1866, all that remained of Colonel Fortescue's kerosene dream was the two stone chimneys and the gaunt outline of the Extractor. Early in World War I, the Extractor was hauled away as scrap to be melted down for the war effort. On Halloween in 1954, the stone chimneys finally toppled to the ground. These stones were later incorporated into the foundation of the Fortescue Beach Palladium. Today all that is left of Persephone's foray into the industrial age is a large square hole in the beach that is filled with lake water and used as a swimming pool. The building that housed the Persephone Bank reopened as a hardware store some years later and was taken over by the Bank of Montreal in the 1960s. To this very day, the Anglican and Presbyterian farmers of the township keep their savings in silver dollars in a sock and form the continent's most challenging market for telemarketers and vacation time-share promoters.

My grandfather provides the epilogue to Fortescue's story.

> Shortly after the Colonel's demise, his widow, Loretta, emerged from her padded room in the northwest tower of Torres Vedras and began giving instructions to the kitchen staff. She made arrangements to have the cigar box containing the great man's ashes interred on the rocky shore where her husband had first warmed himself by a kerosene fire. Before long she was making regular appearances in the shops on Michigan Avenue and had become a

staunch member of the congregation at St. Anne's
Anglican Church. Although much reduced in means,
she was able to arrange the residue of Fortescue's
land holdings to provide herself with a comfortable
income. She lived in the house for another forty
years, having raised two sons and a daughter who
would, in their turns, add new pages to the history of
the Township. She is remembered as the founder of
the Port Petunia Marine Hospital, the chair of the
building campaign for the Imperial Order Daughters
of the Empire Hall, and the author of a number of
charming oil landscapes that now hang in the hospital
boardroom. She died in 1901, the same year as
Queen Victoria, much lamented by her friends, a
pillar of the community and respected by all who
knew her.

As for the legacy of Fortescue and the fate of the township he left in ruins, that is the subject of another chapter.

Scenes like this one took place throughout the Dominion on July 1, 1867, as Canada celebrated Confederation. By this time, the band of the Petunia Valley Foot Regiment had expanded its repertoire from "God Save the Queen" to include the stirring "Prince Consort March."

Chapter 7

THE GREAT SKID
1867 TO 1899

———◆•◆•◆———

A s I was about to begin my research on the late Victorian age in Persephone, my associate Ms. Cameron pressed a weathered copy of a clothbound book into my hands. When I opened the volume to its title page, I read the following: *My Seven Secrets of Success*, by Thomas Patrick Lynch. The book was published in Toronto in 1925.

I already knew something of this son of Persephone from my grandfather's mostly admiring account. "Nothing got by Tom Lynch," was Dr. Goulding's assessment. "If he needed to look surprised about something, he had to practise in front of a mirror for days." My grandfather mentions Lynch's rise in his chapter entitled "The Economic Inactivity of Persephone, 1870 to 1900," but he doesn't delve very deeply into the story.

By the time Lynch's memoirs were published, he'd reached the end of a long and successful career as a businessman, backroom political strategist, and philanthropist. I understand his slim volume inspired a generation of

Persephone schoolboys until one of their teachers noticed the word "damn" on the second page and had the book removed from the shelves. By the time I'd read it through, I'd encountered quite a few more damns. I also knew considerably more about the man who'd dominated the public life of Persephone during the last quarter of the nineteenth century.

Tom Lynch spent only his boyhood and young adulthood in Persephone Township, but he still managed to produce a number of "firsts" for the community. He was the first local financier to die in bed, the first township son to find his way to the Senate, and the first weekender to buy a view property up on the Rift. That he managed these accomplishments without inspiring any torchlight parades says more about his adroit manoeuvring in sticky situations and his eye for the main chance than about any serious business acumen.

Tom's story begins the day he walked out the door of a little cabin up on the Sixth Line and set out to make his fortune in the world. Here is the opening passage from his book.

> On a clear summer day a few weeks after my sixteenth birthday, I walked barefoot down the Old Mail Road from my family's hill farm towards the little village of Larkspur. I carried some clothes in a bedroll and a few dried apples for my lunch and a toothbrush, I think. Nothing more. When I look back on it, that isn't a lot to take with you when you leave home. My inheritance was behind me up on that hill, being a one-tenth share in a hundred acres of blow-sand and a lifetime picking stones. I thought my older brothers could watch over it for me until I really needed it.

The only idea rattling around in my empty head
was to strike out for the bright lights of Port Petunia
and see if I could get a job. I turned out onto the
main road north to the port and before long, I heard
the clip-clop of horses behind me. I turned to see Sam
MacKeown's family from Hall's Corners coming
down the road in a buggy, with the three girls in the
back seat. They were all dressed in their Sunday best,
and there was a big picnic hamper in the wagon box.
Sam and I had spent a few weeks on a team cutting
cordwood for the railways that winter. He pulled up
and offered me a lift into town, and I climbed up with
the picnic basket.

"Great day for it, eh, Tom?" remarked Sam.

"Sure is," I replied, not being certain what the
occasion was. It was a great day for anything, not a
cloud in the sky and three pretty girls leaning over
the back of the buggy seat to make sure I was comfortable. As we trotted along, other wagons joined us
on the road until we formed a little parade. It was the
kind of day that almost made you feel guilty you
weren't out in the field coiling hay. The sky was as
blue as a robin's egg, and the breeze off the lake kept
it from turning hot. The bells started ringing behind
us in Larkspur, and before long we heard the bells
ahead of us in Port Petunia, which was normal enough
for a Sunday morning, but this was a Monday. And
the bells weren't only church bells but every damn bell
in the township.

"Open your eyeballs, lad," said Sam. "Do you not
know what day it is?"

The girls giggled at me sitting there with my
mouth hanging open. For I didn't have the faintest

idea what Sam was talking about. I might as well
have come to town on a load of pumpkins for all I
knew about the world at the age of sixteen. I never
read a newspaper or even looked at a handbill on a
lamppost. I was just as green as grass.

"You're livin' in a new country as of noon today,"
Sam explained. "The bells are ringing to celebrate the
birth of Canada."

It was a pretty poor excuse for a country, I
thought to myself, if the main streets of Port Petunia
and Larkspur were anything to go by. As we got
closer to town, a bunch of yapping dogs joined up
with us, and even they seemed to be in a good mood.
We came round the bend onto Michigan Avenue past
the big Fortescue mansion. Tiles were missing from
the roof and the place badly needed a coat of paint,
but the widow Fortescue was still flying the Union
Jack off the second-floor balcony. The shops along
both sides of the street were closed for the day and
flags hung everywhere. At the far end of Michigan
Avenue, the drydock was empty, but the harbour
beyond it was jammed with logs as far as the eye
could see.

We had just pulled up in front of the town hall
when a "boom" from the breakwall of the harbour
down at the end of the street made the horses jump.
Sam turned and grinned at his wife.

"That'll be the Petunia Valley Foot gettin'
warmed up!" he laughed and looked back at me.
"It's a great day for it, Tom, and you'll be tellin' your
grandchildren you were here the day the country
got borned."

Scenes like the one that Lynch went on to describe were unfolding that day across the four provinces that had joined together in Confederation. John A. Macdonald had announced a day of celebration, and at about the same time Tom stood under the Port Petunia town clock, the new prime minister was receiving a knighthood from the governor general in Ottawa. Had Fortescue lived to see this day, he might finally have elevated himself to the rank of field marshal.

The *Gleaner* describes the crowds on the Port Petunia fairgrounds, with rows of wagons and buggies lined up in the shade of the maple trees, the unharnessed horses munching from nosebags. Families sat on blankets enjoying picnics while the children played games on the common. The Petunia Valley Foot Regimental Band played through the list of entries for the contest to choose a national anthem for the new country, sponsored by the Terpsichore Society. George Gordon Smart's stirring tune "Where Sways the Graceful Elm" was judged the winner by the applause of the crowd. Its refrain: "Ut navis prosilit ecce velum [as the ship leaps forward – behold the sail] / Such is the sight of a graceful el-um."*

Tom describes the speeches of the mayor and his council members as "the only fog seen that day." Harness races churned up the dust on the new racetrack just built by the Persephone Township Agricultural Society. He probably watched the Terpsichoreans re-enact the Great

---

* The song was subsequently recommended to the government as an anthem but no action was taken. George Gordon Smart was disgusted when "The Maple Leaf Forever" became more popular than his song, and he was often heard to mutter loudly at public gatherings when it was sung, "There isn't a single maple leaf west of Winnipeg. What kind of a national symbol is that compared to the sturdy and ubiquitous el-um."

Trek to Larkspur and the coming of the railways to Port Petunia. Maybe he witnessed the premiere of their touching agricultural ballet, *Seeding Time*. At dark he lay on the damp grass with his hands behind his head and watched the stars twinkling in the sky. Chinese lanterns hung everywhere, and a board above the grandstand lit up in a blaze of fire, illuminating a giant maple leaf. And he remembers the fireworks display.

Everybody remembered the fireworks display. Anyone standing within a hundred yards of the wharf that evening had the spectacle burned on the back of their retinas for the rest of their natural lives. George Gordon Smart never forgot it, that's for sure. He immortalized it in a brief poem, his last on a purely Persephone subject.

George Gordon's father, Archie Smart, was by now the leading authority on explosives within a forty-mile radius, but at seventy-two he was beginning to think about retirement. He chose the Confederation fireworks display as his swan song and set to work designing a complex rocket that would climax the show. It was to be fired out of the Crimean War cannon and would carry six star shells into the night sky. As each shell exploded it would illuminate a different letter of the word "CANADA."

Reverberations on the Last Pyrotechnics of Major Smart

He wrote epistles in the skies
And fed upon the children's cries
Of joy and awe and dumb surprise,
A feast of colour for ears and eyes.
One last display,
A last hurrah –
Our first birthday.

For several more verses George Gordon describes the various fireworks leading up to his father's grand finale. The poem then follows Archie as he loads the cannon with his salute to Canada. He had packed the old Russian gun with a triple charge of gunpowder to carry the heavy rocket high into the sky over the harbour. Now he stood before the barrel preparing it for its climactic blast.

Unfortunately, the metal was already fairly hot from its service through the evening. As Archie gingerly nudged the heavy cylindrical rocket down the mouth of the cannon, it must have dislodged a burning ember clinging to the interior. With a crack like thunder the cannon went off.

When the smoke cleared, all that remained of Archie was his boots, sitting side by side in front of the cannon as if he'd just stepped out of them for a moment. Some insisted that they caught a glimpse of him briefly between "C" and "A" in the night sky as the star shells exploded, but this seems pretty far-fetched. Nobody except those next to the explosion really grasped what had happened until the band finished playing "God Save the Queen," and those had been so numbed by the blast that they couldn't speak for a week. But the idea of the artillery expert firing himself into the heavens provided inspiration for the final stanzas of George Gordon's mournful tribute to his father.

> The night that gave our nation birth
> A great soul fled from off this earth.
> As one door opened in our heart,
> Another closed for Major Smart.
> He touched a spark,
> Shattered the dark,
> And left the park.

We'd hoped to lay his dust in sod
But now he's very close to God.
His name is writ in bright, bright hues
Above the clouds in distant views.
Now glory weaves
Immortal wreaths
Upon his sleeves.

The sky gleams bright with fiery stars,
Orion's sword crosses with Mars.
This night of triumph for a nation
Casts Major Smart to his salvation.
He did not choose
To light this fuse –
We have his shoes.

Confederation did not just mark the end of Major Archibald Smart, pioneer, it marked the end of an era for Persephone. Many of the great figures from her early days, like Alexander "the Laird" MacNabb and Colonel Charles Augustus Fortescue, were long gone. Big Sandy had lasted but one term in Ottawa, suffering a fatal stroke when he saw the bill for the new Parliament Buildings. In 1869, only two years after Archie's unfortunate passing, Bertram Haddock was carried off by the chestnut blight. Only Fanny and a handful of others who had made the Great Trek remained.

In his chapter dealing with these years, Dr. Goulding shows little surprise that the great public investments in the railways to Port Petunia failed to bring the expected prosperity to Persephone. At one point he poses the question I have asked myself just about every time I pick up a newspaper: "Why is it that governments so often achieve the exact opposite of what they set out to do?"

The answer in this case is that railways alone do not automatically add value to a community, they just carry materials in and out. And if they carry more goods and people out than they carry in, that place will soon be empty. After the collapse of the Oil Shale Company and the failure of the Persephone Bank, no one in the township could afford to buy much of anything.

Persephone started out with only two natural resources: timber and topsoil. Given the slash-and-burn practices of the day, it is surprising that either lasted as long as it did. The residents watched helplessly as Toronto and Montreal capitalists moved in and bought up the rights to the rich timberlands in the Petunia River Valley that Fortescue had acquired, and which had to be sold at fire sale prices to pay off his debts. In a very short time, decisions for Persephone Township were being made somewhere else.

By 1870, every tree within fifty miles of Port Petunia had been stripped from the hillsides, teamed to the nearest railhead, and shipped off to foreign parts – that is, anywhere east or south of Persephone. The fortunes made in timber, railways, and shipping were sucked away to Toronto and Montreal, although most of the large brick houses on the Upper East Side of Port Petunia date from this period. After a couple of harvests, the topsoil on the cleared ground washed away. With the help of the two railways, the lumber merchants and the farmers drained all of Persephone's riches from her countryside as quickly as water runs out of a bathtub.

The Hog Special and the Fast Freight stumbled from one cash crisis to another until both were insolvent and were finally absorbed into the national Grand Trunk system. When the timber was gone, train service dwindled while freight charges and passenger fares continued to climb. The "great days of the railway" in Persephone were abruptly over, having lasted little more than a decade of steady economic decline and leaving residents with the feeling they get today when the seasons skip directly from winter to summer and spring is left out.

The thirty-nine taverns of the New Military Road, which had been badly hurt by the loss of their overnight guests to the railway hotels in Port Petunia, Larkspur, and Demeter Centre, dwindled to a handful. Some of the hostelries survived as local watering holes, because farmers always need a place to escape the drudgery of farm work. So began that long period of economic and social stagnation that came to be called the "Great Skid."*

Dr. Goulding captures the atmosphere of this period accurately when he writes:

As soon as the sawmills closed, the population began to decline. Whole villages disappeared and many businesses folded their tents. Farm families that were once supported by menfolk moonlighting for the

---

* The Grand Trunk tottered on with massive public support and several illegal loans and was eventually taken over by the federal government in 1919 to form the foundation of Canadian National Railways. By 1917, so much public money had been spent building railways in Canada that Ottawa had to impose the first income tax. The official explanation for the tax was that it was a temporary measure to cover the cost of fighting World War I, but everybody knew the real reason. The income tax was so unpopular that federal politicians of all stripes banded together in a non-partisan coalition to find ways to wipe out the railway and its horrendous expense. Drawing from the example of Persephone, they knew that if they made the service infrequent enough, uncomfortable enough, and expensive enough, people would eventually stop using it. This strategy was applied nationally and by the latter half of the twentieth century, Canada's railways were carrying mostly freight, and not much of that.

lumber companies now found themselves unable to survive on the small crops the land produced. Those who had taken up poor land had to sell and move on. Gradually the character of the community changed. Those high-spirited, brawling Irish and Scottish pioneers who had cleared the land and pummelled the daylights out of each other at every municipal, provincial, and federal election now grew sombre and unyielding in their old age. Their sons and daughters, those who did not limp or lisp or suffer from a fear of heights, packed their belongings in steamer trunks and left for the west or the United States or Toronto, just as their parents had left the stingy soil of the Old Country a generation before. Those who stayed behind soon succumbed to a paralyzing apathy. They became deeply suspicious of new ideas and distrustful of outsiders, regarding the future with uncertainty and not a little fear.

Tom Lynch's journey down to Port Petunia was prompted by economic necessity. As he entered his teenage years, he had watched the daily helpings at the bare plank table in his mother's kitchen grow smaller and smaller. When he announced to his parents that it was time for him to seek his fortune in the world, they raised no objection, and so he joined a growing number of farm boys coming into town from the hills looking for another way to make a living. The "procession of leave-takings" Northrop Frye talked about had begun in Persephone Township, little more than a generation after its founding.

Within a few days of arriving in Port Petunia, Tom bought a pair of second-hand shoes for ten cents and took a job in the Grand Central Hotel serving beer to the patrons. For the next seven years he stood at the bar and listened to the conversations of the human flotsam that washed through the declining port: farmers, merchants, politicians, sea captains, travelling salesmen, and missionaries. He was a good listener and people found it easy to talk to him. One of his regular customers was Lionel Fortescue, younger son of the late colonel, still living with his mother and younger sister in Torres Vedras, in the few rooms not closed off.*

"When I was growing up, the name of Fortescue never came out of a person's mouth up in the highlands without a quantity of spit," Tom wrote. "I wasn't sure Lionel could be someone I would ever like. But he was as friendly as a speckled pup, and he just grew on me like a piece of wild grapevine. It wasn't long till I was going up to the old house and sitting at the big oak table for dinner with his mother and his sister, Madeline."

Tom was also picking up some sound work habits. His memoirs from this period are chock full of simple tricks for getting ahead in life. "I divided my modest salary every month, always remembering to pay myself first with 10 percent regular savings. Then I mailed off a small sum to help my parents on the farm back in Larkspur."

In 1874 the federal government dispatched the new North-West Mounted Police to bring order to the Canadian frontier and police the western border with the United States. Since a cross-Canada railway was still a pipe dream, the only way west was by water. The troops arrived in Port

---

* Reggie had been safely returned from the United States thanks to the intervention of Sir Allan MacNab. He was generally thought to have been an unwitting pawn in his father's manipulations, and he soon became the manager of the Persephone Township Agricultural Society.

Petunia by train, along with several ministers and another load of brooms, and stayed overnight in tents at the fairgrounds. The policemen made quite an impression on Tom and Lionel.

When Lionel and I saw those horses, and the scarlet uniforms and the white helmets, you could have used our mouths for dustpans. They swaggered into the Grand Central, and Lionel and I got behind the bar together to sling drinks at them. Before long we fell into a conversation with the senior officer, Lieutenant Colonel George French, an Irishman who commanded the artillery regiment at Kingston. He said they were short a couple of men and asked if we knew any strong young fellows who could handle a horse. Lionel and I took off our aprons and climbed over the bar to get closer to this gentleman. Next thing we know, he had us by the shoulders. "Why don't you fellas take the Queen's shilling and come with us?"

Lionel busted out the door, ran up the street to Torres Vedras, threw a few things in a bag, kissed his mother and sister, and ran back to the hotel. I think he was gone about nine minutes. I went upstairs and found my toothbrush and I was ready.

At first light the next morning, June 15, 1874, we climbed aboard the steamer loaded with tents, rifles, bedding, flour, lard, horses, and cattle and chugged out of the harbour. As we watched the spires of Port Petunia disappear behind Hawk Island, I turned to Lionel and said, "This is the best view I ever had of Persephone Township. What do you think?" He just grinned at me.

Tom and Lionel represented the latest export of raw material from the township: young people looking for a better life. The Great Persephone Diaspora had begun.

Putting on the Queen's scarlet uniform jolted young Tom out of his Persephone-bred lethargy. When the steamer reached Fort William, every Red River cart in the marketplace was snapped up for military service at twice the going rate. Thousands of dollars of supplies were bought with the stroke of a pen. When a wheel fell off a cart on the horrendous march across the boreal forest of northwestern Ontario, the men tipped the cart off the track and pushed on without a backward glance. Tom watched a beef animal slaughtered every two days to feed the mounted police troop, something that might happen twice a year on the farm back in Persephone. Never before in his life had he seen decisions made so swiftly, such large sums of money spent so casually, and so much waste dropped behind so carelessly. It all had a remarkable effect on the young man. Beneath his crisp white helmet, the brain cells began to percolate and process information. By the time he reached the Red River settlement, he had already settled on his future role in life: as a barnacle fixed firmly to the hull of the ship of state.

In his memoirs Lynch writes about what he learned from his experiences in the west. He and Lionel rode beside Major James Walsh into the armed camp of Sitting Bull and his Sioux warriors, the same Indians who had wiped out General Custer's Seventh Cavalry. He watched Walsh calmly negotiate sanctuary for the Sioux in Canada, riding back and forth between the Indians and the U.S. Army under General Nelson Miles, camped just south of the international boundary line. He also got his first inside look at politics and the exercise of power. After two years of supervising five thousand Indians without a single violent incident, Lieutenant Colonel French was bounced out of his job as commissioner by the Liberal government of Alexander Mackenzie in Ottawa. Tom's comment: "It soon became clear to me that you needed a pretty long spoon to eat out of the same bowl with some people. Standing between a politician and a block of votes was like putting yourself between a cow and her newborn calf."

But Tom quickly developed a sixth sense about where government was going to jump next. "All the good land in Ontario was gone by then, and you didn't have to consult a spiritual medium to see that there would soon be a rush for these fertile plains, with the government doing everything it could to encourage settlement. I had already seen how fast the government will spend money when it takes an interest in a subject. I decided I could do worse than to stand under the coming cash waterfall with a bucket of my own. Money lies all around us on the floor of this great land. All one must do is bend over and pick it up."

And that's just what Tom Lynch did. After three seasons with the North-West Mounted Police, he applied his accumulated pay to the purchase of several strategically placed parcels of land in Saskatchewan and Alberta. Then he took his discharge and made the journey back to Port Petunia, leaving Lionel still toiling happily in the ranks, tearing after the last of the buffalo and drinking up his pay on Saturday nights.

As the steamer bringing Tom home entered Port Petunia harbour, he was confronted with a depressing sight. The drydock stood empty and only two derelict ships were tied up at the wharf. The sawmills were silent and no logs floated in the water. Tufts of grass sprouted out of the roadbed of the railway line. Men lounged on the sidewalks of Michigan Avenue, smoking and staring into space.

In the Grand Central Hotel, Tom ordered his usual glass of strong tea and asked the bartender to explain what was going on. The old man told him that the shipbuilding company was bankrupt and the land had reverted to the town, the timberlands had been cut bare, wheat prices were down, and the brickworks had folded.

Tom downed his tea and went to see the mayor, who turned out to be Lionel's older brother, Reggie Fortescue. Reggie divided his time between the town hall and the race-track at the fairgrounds.

"People have just given up, Tom," said Reggie. "They don't know what to do next."

Tall, tanned, still wearing the uniform of the NWMP, which now hung on his lean frame with calm authority, Tom told Reggie to call a council meeting. In half an hour of straight talk, he persuaded the assembled municipal leaders to give him a twenty-one-year lease on the old drydock for a dollar a year. In return for a ten-year tax holiday, he promised to invest $50,000 in new construction, employing local labour.

Then he took the train to Ottawa, where he convinced the minister of militia of the need for a reliable military connection to Fort William by steamboat until a railway could be built. The minister agreed and financed the refitting of the two derelict steamers in the harbour for $25,000 each. Tom left the construction details in the hands of people he knew from his days behind the bar, then sailed to the lakehead and made a similar proposition to the Fort William Town Council. More contracts soon followed. Within two years he was the chairman of the Great Northern Navigation Company, which led a resurgence of shipping on the Upper Great Lakes.

Soon after his return to Port Petunia, Tom dropped in

to Torres Vedras to call on Lionel and Reggie's younger sister, Madeline. Before long, he and Madeline were engaged. Lionel made it home for the wedding, cutting a dashing figure with his father's lean face and dark eyes. Tom saw his friend's potential and put Lionel's name forward as the Tory candidate in a by-election for the riding of Hillhurst.* A month later, at the age of twenty-seven, Lionel was the new MP, achieving in weeks what had evaded his father at the peak of his power. Either the voters were moved by a strong Christian instinct to forgive past sins, or they had a short memory. I'm not sure it's useful to distinguish between the two.

Through Lionel, Tom met Sir John A. Macdonald and other senior members of the Conservative Party. Tom spent a good part of the winter of 1877-78 in Ottawa, where Sir John and his caucus were serving out the final year of their sentence in opposition for their part in the Pacific Railway Scandal. Comfortably ensconced in a leather chair in the smoking lobby off the House of Commons, drinking dark tea out of a clear bottle (to give the impression of a taste for whisky), Tom schmoozed with Hugh Allan, William Van Horne, a variety of American bankers, and Tory ward-heelers from across the dominion. He spoke quietly and convincingly about the need to encourage new industry through tariffs.

"Erect a 30 percent tariff wall to keep out manufactured imports like cloth, nails, screws, and engines," he told them. "Allow raw materials like cotton, wool, pig iron, sugar, and

---

* Enos Pargeter, who won the seat after Big Sandy's demise in 1867, had died of Rideau Fever, an affliction that strikes new MPs soon after they discover that alcohol and rich food can be charged to their expense accounts. Because of his remarkable constitution, Enos was able to live with the disease for a decade before finally succumbing during the Parliamentary Press Gallery Dominion Day party of 1877.

wheat to come in cheaply, and businessmen will soon see the opportunities for themselves."

Tom's memoirs record the following exchange. Allowing for the inherent untrustworthiness of autobiography, it does have the ring of truth.

"Cheap wheat?" exclaimed Lionel. "But what about the farmers, Tom?"

"Lionel, how many farmers contributed to your campaign?" I asked.

Lionel looked blank and Sir John suddenly burst out in a loud guffaw. His big nose turned bright red with mirth and he said to Lynch in his soft, gravelly voice: "You've hit on it, Tom. The farmer is like the rooster in the hen coop. He makes the most noise and produces no eggs!"

We all had a good laugh over that one and went in for dinner. By midnight the National Policy was born. In the small hours of the morning, I helped Lionel down Metcalfe Street to our boarding house. Lionel turned to me and said, "I thought Sir John was the champion of the farmer. They love him back home, in spite of the mess with the railway."

I explained to Lionel that this was because Sir John always told them what they wanted to hear. "That's the beauty of this country, Lionel. If you want to be the champion of the farmer, all you have to do is stand up on a box and say that you are the champion of the farmer. People will take you at your word. They do not require you to do anything about it."

The following September, the Tories were forgiven by the electorate and returned to office on a platform of high tariffs and support for manufacturing. Five years later, Tom Lynch owned a meat packing plant in Port Petunia, along with a munitions plant, a bridge construction firm, and the Grand Central Hotel, all heavily patronized by various levels of government. He plowed the profits back into more strategically located land purchases in the west. No one was surprised to learn that when the survey of the transcontinental Canadian Pacific Railway was completed, the route passed straight through Tom's landholdings in Saskatchewan and Alberta, which included the future city centres of Regina and Calgary.

In the frenzy of land speculation that accompanied the building of the CPR in the 1880s, Tom Lynch became one of Canada's first paper millionaires. In 1889, at the age of thirty-eight, he turned his paper profits to cold, hard cash, selling everything but the hotel in Port Petunia where he had apprenticed twenty-two years before. With some of his earnings, he bought "Fairlawn," a mansion on Jarvis Street in Toronto, and moved there permanently with Madeline and their five children, all of whom grew up to be disappointments. He accepted directorships on twenty-five different boards and became a member of the Albany Club, the St. George Society, the Knights of Columbus, and the Masons, but he returned every summer to Persephone. He'd moved his aging parents into Larkspur and built a massive fieldstone and timber hunting lodge on the old farm overlooking the Pine River Valley. He loved the magnificent view from the veranda of the lodge, which was marred only by the ramshackle cabin occupied by Fanny Haddock on the next farm and her nomadic goats and chickens.

By this time Tom Lynch was a contributor to more political campaigns than he could count. As the 1880s ended, he began to diversify his contributions, taking a quiet but active interest in the Liberal Party and its new leader, Wilfrid Laurier. "Sir John is not immortal," he warned Lionel on one of the MP's frequent stopovers at Fairlawn on his way home to his constituency. Every fall Tom and Lionel took the CPR back to the Cypress Hills of Saskatchewan to hunt ducks and ride horses over the range they had helped bring order to. Asked once why he never ran for public office himself, Tom said, "There's no sense owning a dog and barking yourself!"

In the summer of 1889, Tom was tending to some business in Toronto when news came from Persephone Township of a terrible calamity. In the middle of the driest summer that anyone could remember, sparks from the stack of the Hog Special started a grass fire just north of Larkspur. The blaze, fanned by a south wind, tore along the riverbanks into Port Petunia, consuming everything in its path. The townspeople fought stoutly, but they were gradually forced back to the harbour, where women and children had already been evacuated into the boats for their safety. By morning, Michigan Avenue was a smoking ruin. The only building left standing on Michigan Avenue was the Grand Central Hotel.

In Toronto, Tom Lynch loaded a boxcar with blankets, food, tents, and medicines, hooked it up to the Fast Freight, and raced to Port Petunia, where he was greeted like a hero. A large crowd escorted him to the hotel he owned and cheered him as he stood on the balcony. He assured them that the town would rise again. The next day he bought both sides of Michigan Avenue for ten cents on the dollar.

In the election of 1891, Sir John A. faced off for the first time against Wilfrid Laurier. Tall, slim, and *très soigné*, Laurier was an unlikely addition to the unrefined atmosphere of the House of Commons. Practically every observer of the day says that he had the soul of a poet and a distaste for the rough-and-tumble of politics as it was then practised. Back in the 1870s, on his first day in the House, he watched in horror as a large book hurled from the opposition benches felled Sir Charles Tupper, a venerable father of Confederation. When Tupper rose shakily to object that he had been hit unfairly without warning, an opposition member scoffed, "It was only the Supplementary Estimates!"

But Tom Lynch could smell change coming and he was anxious to cultivate a younger horse. Macdonald, now seventy-six years old, often stumbled about in an alcoholic haze. The National Policy had won no friends in agriculture, and another reversal in the economy couldn't be far off. All of this was bound to be hard on the governing party.

So Tom hedged his bets, pushing his chips onto Liberal and Tory squares wherever he thought their candidates stood the best chance. His old friend Lionel carried the Tory banner once again for Hillhurst. "They'd vote for a jackass if he were Tory," Tom told him as he signed another hefty donation cheque. "Just smile and keep your head down. In the meantime, Sir John has your name on the list for the Senate if it comes to that."

Both leaders made campaign appearances in the riding. Sir John A., who despite the substance of his policies still played well to an audience of farmers, saw Hillhurst as a seat he should definitely hold. Laurier believed he could rally the progressive vote that had once placed Big Sandy and Enos Pargeter in Parliament and considered it his duty to connect with the considerable "French fact" living in Demeter Township, centred on the village of Rémy-Martin. Laurier came to the riding by train, covering great distances each day in a thoroughly modern style. Sir John opted for a horse-drawn carriage and visited the last three taverns on the New Military Road in a leisurely afternoon's progress, just as if it were 1850.

When Laurier's private rail car pulled into Port Petunia, a respectful crowd was there to welcome him, including, of course, Tom Lynch and Lionel's ever-affable but slightly dissipated older brother, Reggie, now president of the Chamber of Commerce. After the speeches, Tom and Reggie escorted the Liberal leader across the street, sat him down in the saloon of the Grand Central, and handed him a cigar. The subsequent scene makes for one of the most vivid passages in Lynch's memoirs.

> "I'm just a farm boy from the hills up here, Mr. Laurier, and I don't know much about politics. That's your field. But I do know what these people want to hear from you."
>
> Laurier made a shelf of his elegant fingers and rested his chin on it, smiled cautiously at me, and encouraged me to go on.
>
> "They want to know that you understand the natural forces at work in this great country, and they want to see you harness these forces and make them work for their benefit and yours."
>
> "Oh," said Laurier. "And what, pray tell, are these forces you speak of?"
>
> "Racism, bigotry, greed, mawkish loyalty to the Crown, and irrational fear of the United States."
>
> "Oh, dear," said Laurier, looking uncomfortable. "I should like to steer clear of that sort of thing. I want to rise above such matters and concentrate on the great issues of this campaign. If the next century is to belong to Canada, we must break down the

trade barriers with our neighbour to the south. That is the cornerstone of my policy: reciprocity."

I sighed and leaned back in my chair to light a cigar. "Mr. Laurier," I said, "you're a very clever man. And you've got a very, very bright future in this country. But out here in Persephone Township you will find that there are only five things that ever bother the voter when he is trudging around behind a sweaty team of horses and muttering to himself. There's the French, the Catholics, Big Government, and the United States."

"That's four," said Laurier. "What is the fifth?"

"There's always some great Moral Question of the Day that cranks them up. I'm afraid it's temperance again this time."

Laurier's brow furrowed. "These are all sensitive matters which must be handled deftly to preserve harmony in our fragile union. I have devoted all my energies thus far to steering a middle ground, and I am quite confident that I can appeal to the fair-minded in any crowd in the land if I am given the opportunity."

"No one's ever been that interested in the middle ground up here, Mr. Laurier. We think the middle is where everything turns to garbage. So I would forget about that for the moment. Your job, as I see it, is to put the other fellow on the wrong side of each one of these questions. Now, Sir John has made our task pretty easy on the subject of temperance. Then there's the railway mess and his American banking cronies for you to work with. The trick will be to show that he is also soft on the French and playing to the Catholics in some way."

Laurier straightened up in his chair. "Good heavens! Surely you don't mean to say that I am to sully Sir John's reputation with vile rumour and slander?"

"I was hoping to sully it with something more substantial, but rumour and slander will have to do if that's all we've got," I said. "After all, he's going to do the same thing to you."

Laurier pushed back his chair and stood up. "Mr. Lynch, I did not enter politics to play the game you are suggesting. Sir John is an honourable man, and I propose to fight him on the issues alone. On that principle I stand or fall. Good day to you, sir." He turned on his heel and glided elegantly out of the saloon.

I shrugged my shoulders and turned to Reggie. "Such a shame," I said sadly. "That man shows so much promise. He might still make good. We'll have to keep an eye on him."

In the campaign that followed, the Tory strategy team came up with the now famous slogan "The Old Flag, the Old Policy, the Old Leader." Macdonald used the Liberal reciprocity platform to great advantage, taking every opportunity to remind audiences that Laurier was French, Catholic, dangerously sympathetic to the United States, possibly anti-British, and a bit of a dandy to boot.

In his library at Fairlawn, Tom read the reports of the campaign and chuckled to himself. "The old warhorse is as nimble as ever. He hasn't put a foot wrong." Macdonald and the Tories returned to Ottawa with a solid majority, and Laurier found himself once again leader of the opposition. There was no need to put Lionel in the Senate. His appointment would keep for five more years, and so would Tom's.

When I look at the career of Tom Lynch, he appears to be the exception to our thesis that Canada is a land of limited opportunity. He sure didn't settle for 2 to 3 percent real return on his money. But his story actually demonstrates how well the Bliss paradigm performs on the corners as well as on the straightaway. By staying a step ahead of government enthusiasms and market corrections, he was always able to keep his bucket under that cash waterfall. He respected and understood the paradigm, he just refused to be bound by it. He would have agreed with that great backroom strategist Niccolò Machiavelli, who once said, "A man who wants to act virtuously in every way necessarily comes to grief among so many who are not virtuous."

Dr. Goulding reports that Tom Lynch died in bed a happy man. There is a photo of him taken in his drawing room at Fairlawn sometime around the turn of the century, just after he was appointed to the Canadian Senate. He appears to be hugely amused by something. He could afford to be smug. After all, he had kept both feet in the public trough for thirty years, never once risked his own money in private-sector combat, and yet was known across the country as a self-made man. A truly wicked person would have been ashamed to lecture the youth of his day on the magnificence of the free market the way he did.

It is odd that two of Persephone's greatest scoundrels should come to such contrasting ends. Charles Augustus Fortescue had great dreams and an unshakeable belief in his one grand idea. They put him through the Extractor. Tom Lynch had no illusions about anything and no particular beliefs. They put him in the Senate.

The reader may be wondering whatever happened to Fanny Haddock up on the Great Rift. After her husband's untimely demise in 1869, she carried on, according to the principles that now ruled her life: poverty, parsimony, and poetry. The last of these three seems to have blossomed early in her widowhood, perhaps inspired by her nephew's astonishing creative output. For soon after the publication of George Gordon's elegy "Reverberations on the Last Pyrotechnics of Major Smart," her diaries filled up with verse – verse devoid of any discernible syntax and innocent of punctuation. As a later critic, Martin Hunter, would remark, "Fanny was either ahead of her time or out of her mind." I'll let the reader be the judge. I can't make sense of any of it myself.

What regular readers of the Port Petunia *Gleaner* made of Fanny's poetic fantasies is anybody's guess. Every week without fail, under the heading "Rhymes from the Rift" (no rhymes are to be found), a full column was given over to Fanny's explorations of the frontiers of modern literature. I'd wondered how on earth she managed to persuade the paper to publish her stuff until Ms. Cameron started going through Port Petunia's birth, death, and marriage records for the 1870s. Among the entries for 1871 – a respectable four years after Archie's death – she found: "Married – Adelaide Smart, widow, to Horace Bell, publisher." A quick look at the *Gleaner*'s masthead at the time confirmed her suspicions: "Publisher: Horace Bell." (The Bell family's newspaper empire now included more than the Larkspur *Free Press & Economist*, a rare example of a Larkspur business expanding into Port Petunia.) But the crucial clue came a few lines down: "Culture Editor: Adelaide Bell."

Fanny's letters to her sister make no specific mention of Adelaide's role in having her poetry published, but she clearly took great comfort in their correspondence and their shared interest in promoting culture to the residents of

Persephone – whether the residents wanted it or not. Adelaide finally succumbed to a nagging pneumonia in 1895, leaving Fanny the matriarch of a large extended family. (The younger Haddocks had taken up land at the south end of Persephone, deep into the highlands and on a different mail route, where they learned low-impact agriculture: a combination of pasture farming, distilling, and bass fishing.) Her weekly column in the *Gleaner* ends the same year, but she continued to write: diaries, stacks of letters to her children, short stories, a novel about the death of her dog, and poetry – reams and reams of poetry.

Only recently has Fanny Haddock's true contribution to Canadian literature started to become clear. Another literary critic, P.C.L. Timmerman, says, "Haddock invented the interior monologue and created the distinctive Canadian voice of quiet realism. It is a voice that speaks to us from a bare cabin on an exposed drumlin in the middle of February with the wind howling through the chinks between the logs. It tells us of wilted crops, failed men, disappointing children and the implacable hand of a malicious deity. If the reader was ever of the opinion that things could be worse, he need only pick up a volume of Fanny Haddock to confirm his fears."

No, Fanny's legacy cannot be measured in the same terms that her neighbours used to gauge success: by acres cleared, bushels of wheat grown, and mortgages paid off. The crowning achievement of her life was her writing, the popularity of which eventually spread beyond the borders of Persephone. For every reader puzzled by Fanny's insistence on exploring the inner life of trees – "Who wants to read this dreary crap?" wrote one male reviewer in *Saturday Night* (1887) – there were ten who hailed her as an unsung genius of the backwoods.

By the time Fanny entered her eighties, students of Canadian literature and many recognized literary figures were making the pilgrimage to Larkspur every year, there to sit on a stump in the little clearing – one of the nine stumps her late husband had managed to leave as his legacy – and listen to Fanny recite her now celebrated "The Death of a Dog in Late Winter." When she saw other, younger people – Pauline Johnson, Bliss Carman, Archibald Lampman, Ernest Thompson Seton, and, of course, her very own nephew George Gordon Smart – go on to occupy centre stage in Canadian literary life, she was philosophic. She seemed to take a simple pride that she had touched their lives.

On a bright summer day in the summer of 1899, the year she turned eighty-eight, Fanny Haddock could be found, as usual, kneeling in her garden. The strawberries needed attention. She was the last living member of the original group of MacNabb pioneers who had made the Great Trek in the summer of 1833, but still spry enough to be "up and doing" every day, as she had done all her life. She still lived in the tiny log cabin that had been her home when the pine forest once towered around Larkspur like the walls of a canyon. She didn't know it, but the dominion government was set to announce one week later that a small fund had been established for her by a group of admiring benefactors.

Apart from her large garden and a little flock of goats, her family's attempts at taming the wilderness had been a flat failure. Fanny lived on goat's milk, goat cheese, berries, fish, and the odd fool hen that wandered within range of her shotgun. She was a genius at scavenging edibles from the fencerows and the ditches. Most pioneers had graduated from this kind of life after ten or fifteen years, but Fanny had managed to stretch it out for the better part of three generations. In this climate of deprivation it is under-standable that all of her children left home early, made unhappy marriages, and effected the first divorces among the families of the township.

Had Fanny glanced up, she might have seen all this and written a poem about it. Instead, she keeled over face down in the strawberry patch and breathed her last. She was dis-covered by a young poetess from Toronto come to visit her muse. Those who attended the memorial service in the Larkspur church remarked how peaceful Fanny looked after nearly a century of toil.

On the north wall of the nave of St. Luke's Anglican Church in Larkspur, about halfway back, there are twin stained glass windows dedicated to Fanny and her sister, Adelaide. One shows St. Luke, the physician and classi-cally trained writer, hauling empty nets into a boat. The other portrays St. John, "The Favoured One," pining away on a rock in exile on the island of Patmos, feeding the birds and writing Revelations. The motto underneath the two windows advises the reader: "Go thou and do likewise."

"Fanny was an unlikely pioneer," says Dr. Goulding in the chapter that brings his examination of the nineteenth century to a close. "But she adapted to her surroundings with the same determination with which the gnarled and ancient cedars cling to the rock face of the Rift, taking nourishment from only the rain and dust hurled at them by the relentless winds that swirl among the heights."

Reading this passage made me reflect that this is true for so many of the characters who made their way through the annals of Persephone's early days. For better or worse, they were all shaped by the rugged and unforgiving land-scape. And they survived.

Many of the sons of Persephone answered the call to serve overseas in World War I. Here young recruits wait on the Larkspur station platform for the train that will take them off to war in September 1914. Fewer than one in four would return.

Chapter 8

INTO THE TRENCHES
1900 TO 1929

———◦•◆•◦———

In his chapter titled "The Modern Era," Dr. Goulding paints a picture of a community that has dwindled into calm resignation at its fate as a quiet backwater in the Ontario countryside.

As the twentieth century dawned, it seemed the world had simply passed Persephone by, that her moment of greatness, such as it was, had faded into the fog that so often descended on the deserted wharves of Port Petunia Harbour. As the rest of Canada went from strength to strength, Persephone and the adjacent townships in Hillhurst County entered the fourth decade of the Great Skid. Larkspur's population dropped to two hundred and the Port Petunia factories founded by Tom Lynch (and sold off by him at a handsome profit) closed their doors. The drydock dwindled back into a repair shop for the faltering shipping industry. Topsoil ran down the hillsides of the highlands and blew off the treeless flats of Demeter.

As I tackled the new century in Persephone, I found myself in a new working environment as well. Ms. Cameron never approved of my work station at the bar in the Commercial Hotel, and she set me up in a cubicle of the library. Thereafter she just wheeled in a cart with the day's reading material on it and I wheeled it back to her when I was finished. My productivity has always been higher when I am supervised.

The September 1910 Progress Edition of the Larkspur *Free Press & Economist* had meagre progress to report: "A highlight of the year was a very fine hog produced by William McCannel of Victoria Street weighing 550 pounds dressed and only two years old. Mr. McCannel says the hog already weighed 450 pounds when it was a year old and should have reached 800 pounds, but 'it had run down some during the summer.'"

And so things might have continued, but for faraway events. On June 28, 1914, a crazed Serbian nationalist fired a pistol at an overdressed aristocrat showing the flag for the Austro-Hungarian Empire on a visit to Sarajevo, and the noise woke up Persephone. When Great Britain declared war on Germany, Persephone's sons volunteered in droves: the war gave them the first prospect in their short lives of a paying job.

One of these volunteers was Kernel Albert Hall, great-grandson of the Amos Hall who had made the Great Trek with an orphan named Hector strapped into a cradle in the wagon box and whose descendants still wouldn't speak to a Pargeter. Kernel Hall, it turns out, was a great-uncle to Ms.

Cameron, and she has provided quite a few details that help fill in his background.

In the early 1890s the family farm on Hall's Hill had passed to Amos's grandson, Jack Hall, and his wife, Nellie (*née* Clark). Nellie had come to Larkspur from Toronto in 1886, the year after the Great Fire, to teach in the new brick schoolhouse. Nellie was what people in those days referred to as a "free thinker," a label the church elders and the school boards of the time pinned on any woman with an opinion that differed from their own. This was a step forward from "heretic" or "heap of chaff" and represented progress of a sort. Jack had had so much religion stuffed into him at the dinner table by his parents and grandparents that he'd completely lost his appetite for it, which didn't bother Nellie. When Jack proposed to her on a swing in the schoolyard, he told her that he had dwindled to a "congregation of one" and would observe the Sabbath on his knees in the vegetable garden if she didn't mind. She accepted his proposal.

When their first child arrived, Jack took the baby in his arms and exclaimed that he was "no bigger than a kernel of corn." Nellie laughed and for the first few weeks they called the baby "the Kernel." Jack raised no objection when she drove the infant in the buggy down Hall's Road to St. Luke's one Sunday and had him christened Kernel Albert Hall. The boy preferred "Albert," but his schoolmates latched onto "Kernel," and after three or four fistfights in the mud, they learned to say it without sneering. According to the custom of the day, Nellie gave up teaching once she was married, but it appears she found an outlet for her didactic instincts in the upbringing of Kernel and her second child, Louise, who was born three years later. She read to both children from the classics and the myths, taught them to play on the upright piano she'd brought from Toronto, and made them memorize long passages from Shakespeare, Wordsworth, Blake, and a new poet, A.E. Housman.

In August 1914, when the news of war reached the Halls' farm kitchen, Kernel was twenty-six years old. There was very little discussion that day. There seldom was at the most serious moments in the Hall household. Nellie packed a bag for her son and placed in it a dozen pairs of home-made underwear, *The Book of Common Prayer*, *The Oxford Book of English Verse*, a volume of Shakespeare's tragedies, and *A Shropshire Lad*. His father sat on the veranda smoking quietly until it was time to harness the horse and make the trip down Hall's Road to the station. In my grandfather's words, "Kernel bid farewell to his parents and boarded the Hog Special with twenty other boisterous young men from Persephone, boys with names like Cameron, Fisher, MacNab, Haddock, MacKelvey, Bell, and Pargeter. Few would return."

There is a distinct shift of focus in this final chapter of Dr. Goulding's pioneering work. He abandons his lofty contemplation of communal history to focus on one family, the Halls, and in particular on Kernel. But once Kernel and his mates have boarded the train for Newmarket, where they would formally enlist before being shipped off to Valcartier, Quebec, for "basic training," my grandfather's account becomes more distanced. He runs down the list of the major battles of the war like a shopping list, in a single paragraph that simply notes the recruits from Persephone wounded or killed in each engagement. At the end of the war, he reprints the honour rolls from the cenotaphs in Larkspur and Port Petunia. That's it. There are a few para-graphs of material to round out the chapter and the book;

these pages are heavily water-damaged but seem to bear little relationship to what has gone before. They may deal with the post-war influenza epidemic, but it's difficult to say. Within a few pages he goes on to tell the story of Persephone in the 1920s.

As far as I can remember, my grandfather never spoke about his own experiences in the war. If he had, I probably wouldn't have paid much attention.* In fact, tackling this chapter proved to be something of an ordeal for someone as ignorant of military matters as myself. I sat for hours staring out the window, wondering if I should just bring the book to a halt with the death of Fanny Haddock. When I mentioned my problem during a telephone conversation with Ms. Cameron, she asked me when I might next be free for lunch at the Red Hen. I flipped through my schedule book and found an opening the same day at one o'clock.

"I wonder what Dr. Goulding did during the war," I mused as we both scraped the gravy off our hot beef sandwiches. "He was only a few years younger than Kernel Hall, so he would certainly have been old enough to serve."

Ms. Cameron pulled a fat manila envelope out of her shoulder bag and slid it across the table with a slightly embarrassed smile. "I don't have an answer to that question," she said, "but this may help you finish the chapter." I opened the envelope and removed its contents.

I was staring at a stack of handwritten letters. The top letter was written in a firm bold hand, dated September 21, 1914, and began, "Dearest Mother." I quickly turned it

* I think my aversion to matters military can be traced to the time I served as a member of the ship's band in the Sea Cadet Corps at school. I was very nearly lost at sea during a war game exercise on Whitefish Lake, when I fell overboard with my baritone tuba. We won the war game and I was decorated posthumously.

over to read the signature: "Your devoted son, Kernel." The next letter, dated a week later from Larkspur, was signed, "Your loving mother."

I looked at the attractive woman sitting opposite.

"This is quite a find. Where'd you come across these?"

"Oh, I've known about them for a while. They cover the whole period Kernel was in the Canadian Expeditionary Force, from the time he left Larkspur until . . . but I'll let you read them yourself. He was at Vimy Ridge, you know."

"Why didn't you tell me about them before now?"

"Well, I wasn't sure if you would know what to do with them. But now . . . I think you do."

The letters had come into Doreen Cameron's possession from her grandfather, who'd gotten them from his sister, who, it seemed, had married Kernel Hall. (If you spend much time in Persephone, you'll soon start to believe that if you just go back far enough, everybody is related to everybody.) Although parts of Kernel's letters were blacked out by the censors and some of Nellie's letters seem to have been lost – not surprising given the conditions the troops faced in the trenches – together they tell the story of how Persephone went to war and how the war came back to Persephone. Because these letters speak for themselves, I have reproduced them here with a minimum of comment, deleting only those items irrelevant to the story. His first letter was written from Valcartier, Quebec, even though he pretends he has already crossed the ocean.

September 21, 1914
Dearest Mother,

I am not allowed to tell you where we are stationed lest I give our position away to the enemy. All

I am supposed to say is that we are in good health, have plenty to eat, and our spirits are excellent.

The Germans are unlikely to come anywhere near us in these conditions. The camp is a sea of mud and confusion. There aren't enough tents, uniforms, and boots, and no one has any idea what we are supposed to be doing. The only article available in good supply is the local whisky stilled by the farmers of the area, but I assure you that I know better than to yield to its temptations.

We joined to serve the Empire, but it appears the Empire has no great need for us at present. We do get plenty of exercise. They fed us a very old pig yesterday and Stubby MacNab reacted by redecorating the mess hall with it. Then he set fire to his tent. They will have to send in someone who can manage us soon or we will not be much use to anyone.

Kiss Louise for me,

Your devoted son,

Kernel

The next letter in the cache was sent in late November soon after Kernel's arrival at the great training camp on England's Salisbury Plain. It refers obliquely to a "turbulent crossing," which, according to other accounts, did not have anything to do with the weather. The conditions were so bad on board that the Canadian recruits ran amok once again, destroying the ship's canteen and pitching government property over the side. According to Ms. Cameron, the story goes that the boys of Persephone broke into the stores in the hold during the voyage and looted the supplies of a western cavalry regiment. When they finally spilled off the ships in Southampton, they were all wearing spurs, and a British adjutant assigned them to the Mounted Rifles. In Southampton they promptly went AWOL, probably to the nearest pub. The letter concludes:

> We were finally gathered up by the military police and delivered to another mud-choked wasteland where nobody knows what they are doing. Our brigade commander is a thick-shouldered man with gigantic veins on his nose. He is clearly embarrassed at being assigned the temporary charge of Dominion troops. He rides about hurling insults at us as we tramp back and forth in the mud. You will be pleased to know that we have mastered the art of forming a British square, a battlefield tactic that was very effective at Waterloo.
>
> The manufacturers of our Canadian-made equipment have probably lined their pockets, but most of it is perfectly useless for conditions here. We have been issued an excellent target rifle, but it tends to jam after three or four shots. The wind goes straight through the thin cotton cloth of our uniforms, and water seeps into our boots after three steps in the mud.
>
> They tell us if we don't behave, we shall be broken up and farmed out to other divisions, but I don't know who would have us.
>
> I will stop whinging now and go shovel the snow off the roof of my tent. Do we have enough hay to last till spring? I'm now starting to wonder if I will be home for the planting. Write soon with any news.
>
> Your devoted son,
> Kernel

Nellie's first letter caught up to Kernel on Salisbury Plain, where he was still in training.

December 31, 1914
Dear Kernel,

We are so pleased to hear that you are safe. We got your letters all in a bundle this morning and Louise, your Father, and I have been devouring them all day. We have been so worried about you, especially knowing the damp conditions you have had to endure and the poor quality of your equipment.

The newspapers are full of questions about the way we are supporting the troops, and we are doing our best here in Larkspur to make your life a little brighter. The women of the church have formed a group to put packages together for you. I hope you got the ones we sent in time for Christmas. We are sending another parcel tomorrow that contains socks and underwear and gloves. But you must write as soon as possible and tell us what you need.

Your father has done an excellent job of preparing us for winter. We have lots of wood and forage to last us and the air is crisp and dry – just the sort of winter you and your Father consider healthy for "man and beast."

I will close now because I am going to the church to take the decorations down for the New Year's service.

Don't worry about us.

Your loving mother.

P.S. Try to keep your feet dry.

Kernel made it to France with the first contingent of Canadians and was introduced to the horrors of trench warfare in the second battle of Ypres, in April of 1915. Over the next eighteen months he saw action at the Somme, Festubert, and Givenchy. By the end of 1916, the war had degenerated into a hopeless stalemate along a two-hundred-mile front that extended from the North Sea to the border of Switzerland.

Throughout this period, mother and son wrote faithfully to each other. As conditions worsened and losses mounted, their letters paradoxically become more resolutely cheerful.

December 12, 1916
Dearest Mother,

I'm writing this letter by the light of a candle in an old shoe polish tin, so I hope you will excuse the poor penmanship. Stu Fisher and I just took advantage of the lull in the proceedings to go for a bit of a stroll in No-Man's Land, and now we are settling into our cots for some rest. It's very quiet in our section of the front, and we enjoy sitting up on deck chairs in the evening in our greatcoats, watching the Very light flares popping up from the other side. A lot like the Larkspur fairgrounds on the Queen's Birthday.

You really mustn't worry about me, Mother. Fritz is a terrible shot and we have a great laugh holding up barn doors to see if he can hit one. The grub is certainly not up to your standards, but there's lots of it and plenty of good English tea to wash it down. I'm keeping up with my reading, just as I promised you I would do. Stu and I performed the "Once more into the breach" scene from *Henry V* for our platoon, and they are unanimous that we will make our fortunes on the stage when the war is over. Headquarters gives us armfuls of uplifting material to read and a

stint in the library once a week if we keep our
buttons polished and our boots shined.

If you have any news of any of the other boys
from Persephone, please pass it along. We have been
bounced about over the last six months and have lost
track of Stubby MacNab, Henry Haddock, Leonard
Bell, and others. But we're in a quiet spot now, knit-
ting ourselves new socks and straightening up the
barracks, so life is quite agreeable. Wim Cameron
and Stu and I have managed to hang together
through all of it, which has been quite a trick, really.
You'll be pleased to hear that I'm a lieutenant now
and Stu and Wim are both sergeants, but we [the
lines following have been blacked out].

Tell Father to keep packing those parcels for the
Mounted Rifles. We especially enjoyed that very
strong tea he sent last time. It seems to do wonders
for our singing voices.

Bit of a bump just came on the roof. I'll sign off
before we lose the lights.

Your devoted son,
Kernel

That Kernel, Stu, and Wim were still together after a
year and a half at the front was more than "a trick," it was
a miracle. The Mounted Rifles had been badly cut up
during the Battle of the Somme in July and August 1916,
losing much of their fighting strength. And the idea that
Kernel and Stu were out "for a bit of a stroll" in no man's
land is absurd. He's obviously referring to a night patrol,
which was often the safest way to pass the night – a lot safer
than sentry duty, when you had to sit stock still with just
your head above the parapet.

I pick up the correspondence two years after Kernel's first Christmas in the army and with the war nowhere near resolution.

December 26, 1916
Dear Kernel:

At last we have received a letter from you, weeks after you had written it, but it did arrive in time for Christmas Day, thanks to Peter MacNab, who walked up through the drifts in filthy weather to see that we received it. He asked me to pass along greetings from Stubby, who has been sending the odd postcard.

I hope you are keeping up your reading. Books are windows on the world and have always been my greatest joy when I have something on my mind that won't go away, like how to make you attend to your lessons or how to make Louise do her chores. You have a great spirit in you, and I am so proud that despite the vicissitudes of the past two years, you have not sought refuge in any of the vices that are so freely available to men in arms. I know you are smiling as you read this, and I assure you I am not as innocent as you think. I spent enough time with young boys in the backwoods as a teacher, and I know what they get up to when they are left to their own devices.

As promised, we sold much of the livestock in the fall. Already it is proving to have been a good plan, because your father can sit and watch the storms instead of shovelling a path both ways to the barn the way the two of you used to do together. He has kept back three of your best black heifers and plans to put Sovereign in with them in June. They are most

promising animals and he shows them to anyone who
comes in the yard to visit. He is proud as punch to
tell people they are the first Angus cattle in
Persephone and that you were the one who insisted
we get them.

Premier Hearst came to Larkspur in November.
He made all sorts of jokes that no one laughed at, and
he said many silly things about defending our
Christian way of life that made Father snort loudly
and brought all heads around to look at him. I think
even Mr. Hearst must know that, by now, most families just want their boys out of it and safe home. They
say he has a couple of boys overseas himself.

Louise has been home over Christmas but is due
back in the city in a day or two. She is doing splen-
didly in Toronto, having found a position working in
the general hospital, which puts great demands on
her energy but gives her the satisfaction of contribut-
ing to the war effort. (In response to the mention you
made about your singing, she asks whether your
superior officers have considered using it to frighten
off the Germans!)

Take care of yourself and know that my prayers
are with you every hour. In his own way, so are your
father's.

Your loving,
Mother

P.S. Your Father assures me that he will soon be dis-
patching another package of comestibles, including
more of that special tea you are always enquiring
after. Every time I offer to buy it for him, he changes
the subject.

Like her son's, Nellie's letters were written in a kind of code. Stubby MacNab was not "sending the odd postcard." He'd been listed as missing since the previous summer.

Early in January 1917, Kernel Hall's company marched north to the Artois sector along with the other contingents in the Canadian Mounted Rifles. Between Loos in the north and Arras in the south, they moved into trenches in front of the French town of Thelus, at the base of a long rising slope named Vimy Ridge. They were there for a rest, to put themselves back together again like many other divisions, after the mauling they had taken at Givenchy and Festubert.

This was one of the most heavily fortified positions on the Western Front, held by the Germans since the very beginning of the war. Nearly a quarter of a million French and British men had been lost trying to take that ridge, and both the Allied and the German commands had come to the conclusion that it was impregnable.

Jan. 15, 1917

Dearest Mother:

Just in from a brilliant action led by Lieutenant Kernel Hall, ably supported by his two sergeants. You will probably read about it shortly in official dispatches in the *Free Press*. Under cover of darkness and without any supporting artillery, these heroic men of Persephone rushed a French henhouse well behind our lines and came away with a dozen eggs. The defenders were caught completely unprepared and there were no casualties. I have put Wim and Stu through for their DSOs – Delivering Superb Omelettes – and our triumph is being celebrated up and down the line as a first for the Canadians. As usual the British are taking complete credit for the operation and the French are upset, asking why we didn't bring back the hens.

I got your Christmas letter this morning. It made me terribly homesick to think of you and Father and Louise gathered around the spindly pine tree that Father always harvests from the roadside and that you drape with the same handful of tinsel that you had as a little girl. I miss the smell of Father's pipe and the oranges in the stockings and Louise opening all my presents for me. Give her a big hug and tell her that all the boys here who have seen her photo have come down with a sudden fever and asked to be taken straight to the Toronto General.

Things are much changed for us since rejoining the Canadian Corps. When I came in from one of my evening walks [Kernel was still drawing night patrols] last night, Wim came up and whispered to me that the captain wanted to see me. I made my way along the trench in the dark, when one of those silly little mortars crashed into the parapet up ahead of me. Generally they come in twos and threes, so I ducked into the dugout entrance and started double-time down the steps in the dark. At the halfway point another shell exploded on the roof. The effect was like a blow between the shoulder blades with a baseball bat. It knocked me down the last twenty steps to the bottom, where a blanket soaked in vermoral spray solution hung across the doorway to keep nasty odours [likely a reference to mustard gas] from entering the dugout. I somersaulted through the doorway, tearing the blanket off its hooks, and sprawled onto the floor, still in absolute darkness. As I sat up and felt myself for broken bones, an officer calmly relit the candles on the little plank table. Another helped me to a bench and stuck a mug in my hand containing half an inch of very strong tea. This was Lieutenant Colonel Muirhead, our battalion commander.

"Who do we have here?" asked a voice at the table.

"Kernel Hall," I said, shakily.

"Colonel?" said another voice with an English accent from behind the table. I could see he was wearing red tabs on his collar. "Have you been hiding one from me, Arthur?"

"That's his Christian name," said the captain.

The next thing I registered was that the portly officer at the table had red tabs, as well. It was old Guts and Gaiters, General Arthur Currie, the divisional commander. He's a good man and all the fellows admire him. Very careful with us and doesn't rush into anything. But he does look most unmilitary. Unlike the other fellow, the one with the Brit accent. I'm afraid I lost my temper for a bit and said something mocking about how the men were itching to have another crack at Fritz. It must have been the shock from the mortar or the cup of black tea they gave me to settle me down.

"This is your corps commander," said Captain Muirhead sternly and introduced me to General Sir Julian Byng. I'm sure you'll have read of him from the Gallipoli reports. He brought eighty-three thousand men safely off the peninsula at Suvla without a single casualty, apart from one fellow with a broken leg, and I think they drowned a mule. I'm told he went to Eton with the King. Apparently his school chums call him "Bungo."

"Well, this bird's a long way from his wine cellar,"
I thought, never, ever having seen a corps commander this close to the front line. I tried to salute,
but Sir Julian just lifted his hand, still in his pocket,
and said, "Never mind that."

Next thing I knew, he was questioning me closely
and we were deep in discussion, as if I were a corps
commander instead of a lowly lieutenant. I told him I
would have thought even Sir Douglas Haig, our
supreme commander, would be tired of frontal assaults
on heavily fortified positions by now. I could feel the
toe of the captain's boot coming in my direction again,
but Sir Julian held up his pocket once more.

"Yes, absolutely right," he said. "We're bloody
tired of it, and we think it's time to rethink a lot of
things." I got the impression he doesn't think much of
Sir Douglas. Anyway he suddenly turned to Currie
and said: "Here's another one, Arthur," and they gave
me a new job. They have put me in a nice safe spot so
far from the guns that the hens are laying eggs. It's all
first names and "As you were, Kernel," as if I were
working for the township road crew. I'd be quite
happy to spend the rest of the war right here.

Tell father not to put Sovereign on my heifers
because he is too big for them just yet. I told you that
you should have sent my heifers out when you sold
the others. I know he wants to have some purebred
calves for me when I come home, but it would be
safer to put them to the Camerons' little Hereford
bull this year if he is determined to keep them. There
will be lots of time to build up the herd when I come
back. And tell him June is much too early for breeding
them. I would worry about him trying to get calves to

suck in the mud and wind of March. He should be sitting by the fire then and waiting until the buds come out and the breeze is warm. Tell him I shall be very cross with him if I hear he has been fighting with late winter calves.

Your devoted son,

Kernel

P.S. By the way, Father's tea is wildly popular with the men. And sorely missed. The last shipment – a six-month ration of this precious substance – went down in the Channel. Our nerves have been on edge. None of the other mothers seem able to get their hands on this particular brand, so we particularly look forward to Father's packages. Give Father my best and scratch Sovereign over the withers for me.

How that letter got past the censors is anybody's guess. I suppose they couldn't read everything. Kernel's next letter to his mother hints at the enormous preparations for the Vimy assault.

March 1, 1917

Dearest Mother:

We are busier now than at any time I can remember and morale is very high. I know I sound like a recruiting poster, but there has been a great change in the ranks here since we came up to this spot. The Canadians are all together and we are working to a common purpose with our own officers for the first time.

I'm working with a great fellow from Montreal who keeps a lion cub under his desk. He sends me out each night with Wim and Stu to do odd jobs, and

we are seeing a great deal of the front. It's not particularly dangerous work because Fritz is convinced we
haven't got the jam in us for another serious fight,
and he leaves us pretty much alone.

    Your devoted son,

    Kernel

The man with the lion under his desk was Andrew
McNaughton, an engineer from McGill University and
the best artillery mind in the Allied army. I remember my
history teacher telling us how McNaughton pioneered
the technique of "sound ranging," which could pinpoint
enemy heavy guns as much as five miles behind the lines.
Kernel's "odd jobs" were probably setting up and staffing
McNaughton's listening posts in no man's land, each
equipped with telephones and survey equipment. Through
the day, men crouched in the forward posts, listening to the
bangs of the guns and reporting to McNaughton and the
artillery. By the end of March, McNaughton had identified
the positions of all the German heavy field guns and could
locate a new one within a few minutes.

According to what I've read, after the disaster of the
Somme, the commanders of the Canadian Corps abandoned
the idea of massed infantry assaults on heavily fortified positions and returned to the platoon system of "fire and movement." An exact replica of the Vimy front was laid out
behind the lines. Coloured pennants outlined the enemy
roads, dugouts, machine guns, pillboxes, and barbed wire
entanglements. For the first time, each soldier was given a
map and a specific responsibility. In three months, the
Canadians built twenty-five miles of roads, nineteen miles of
light railway, forty-four miles of water pipe, and ninety-four
miles of signal wire. They made twelve tunnels up to the

lines in the limestone cliffs to deliver the men to the front under cover. One of the tunnels alone could hide a thousand men. When preparations were complete, 983 guns were aimed at the ridge, plus another 150 machine guns that would send a storm of bullets to harass the German rear. It was to be the most elaborately planned, carefully executed assault in the entire war.

March 21, 1917
Dearest Mother:

Sorry this note is so brief, but we barely have the time to sit down and eat these days. Tell Father his latest tea shipment came through, and it has caused more rejoicing in this sector than any military news all winter. Sir Julian says that Father has made an enormous contribution to the war effort and should be mentioned in dispatches.

Everything we do infuriates the Brits. They're calling us Byng's Boys, and it isn't a compliment. But I wouldn't trade my place here for anywhere else in the army.

I must be off to run an errand for Andy.
All my love,
Kernel

By this time, Nellie had finally received Kernel's letter from the previous December with news of his promotion to lieutenant.

March 25, 1917
Dear Kernel:

Your letter arrived by the morning post and we were so pleased to hear that you are feeling more yourself. It must be the promotion that is lifting your spirits. Father says the last officer in the Hall family fought in the Monmouth Rebellion against Charles II more than two hundred years ago, on the wrong side, of course. You know your father's family.

Louise is coming home at the end of April to help your father get the spring grain in. I thought your father might have been too proud to let her drive a team, but he laughed and said, "I will go out and tell Bud and Polly right away. They will be so pleased not to have me to pull around this year." You are always in our thoughts and the Cameron girls, Ada and Sarah, ask to be remembered to you, as well. Try not to forget your reading, busy as you are. It keeps your mind supple and open to new ideas. Take good care of yourself.

Your loving,
Mother

Nellie didn't mention that Henry Haddock had died in a hospital in England at the beginning of February, apparently from an infection that developed from his wounds. Nor did she tell him about the black-bordered telegram that had arrived at Stubby MacNab's parents' farm, or how Stubby's father now spent the winter days sitting in a chair in the front room, speaking to no one.

As the snow melted and the grass sprouted on the Western Front, Kernel wrote another letter to his mother.

April 2, 1917
Dearest Mother,

Spring is in the air and as always, it makes me impatient to be in the fields. The ground in this part of France is heavy clay and dries slowly, much like our front field at home. I smile when I imagine Father watching the farmers down in the Valley working the fine loam of the flats. He bangs his pipe on the veranda rail, and I can hear him scolding me, "Don't watch the other fellows down there in the sand. Our ground's not the same. If you work it now, you'll have clumps as hard as rock and they'll be there for three years. Go on away with you for at least a week."

As if I would leave Hall's Hill to let him fret by himself! But then the day comes when the earth crumbles through his fingers like short pastry dough from your kitchen, and he grins and says, "Are you ready for work, Kernel?" Three passes with a cultivator and it makes a seedbed so fine and soft you could lie down on it and go to sleep.

Your devoted son,
Kernel

On April 2, the day Kernel wrote this letter, the Allied guns along the Western Front opened up, and for the next seven days, a million high explosive shells rained down on the German fortifications. One of the books about Vimy I've read claims that some of the explosions were heard by the British prime minister in London as he stood out in front of his residence on Downing Street. By the end of the week, McNaughton's team had knocked out more than 80 percent of the German field guns.

On Easter Monday, April 8, 1917, the Arras offensive opened across a forty-mile front with combined assaults by the French in the south, the British in the north, and the Canadians in the centre. Four Canadian divisions attacked up Vimy Ridge, the only time in our history that the entire Canadian Corps would see action together on the same day.

Ms. Cameron and I have been able to reconstruct something of Kernel's part in that day because he was finally, after all his offhand treatment of his own bravery, mentioned in the official dispatches.

> Lt. K.A. Hall and two sergeants led a party of rifle grenadiers behind a gun emplacement and put it out of action sustaining heavy loss. With both sergeants seriously wounded, Hall continued forward under fire with his remaining men, driving on to his objective, pushing the enemy over the edge of the ridge and holding it until relieved.

At this point in his account, Dr. Goulding departs from his laundry list of battles to record Kernel's winning of the Military Cross and to summarize the remarkable accomplishment of the Canadian Corps that day.

> In the brave assault on Vimy Ridge, 3,598 Canadians died and another 7,000 were wounded. The Canadians penetrated further than any other division in two and a half years of trench warfare. For the first time in the long and bloody conflict, German siege guns were captured. Vimy remained firmly in Allied hands until the end of the war. Fourteen men and boys from Hillhurst County are buried in the war cemetery near the Vimy monument, and dozens more brought home permanent scars. Sergeant Wim Cameron died of his wounds in a French hospital. Sergeant Stu Fisher lost his hand and made it home.

Kernel Hall emerged from the Vimy action a major and carried on with the Second Division, watching the tactics learned at Vimy spread throughout the Allied army. He led his company of the Mounted Rifles through the pillboxes and bunkers and the mud of Third Ypres and the battle for Passchendaele. At Christmas, General Currie promoted him to lieutenant colonel, because his men "had been calling him that for months anyway." In January, a shell splinter shattered his hip and ended his war.

The last two letters between Kernel and his mother were both written the day of the Armistice and crossed in the mail.

November 11, 1918
Dearest Mother:

A group of us heard the news in the garden of a converted country house in Suffolk, where I have been playing croquet in the rain for the last month. Not a pastime that would catch on in Persephone. It requires too much flat ground. I am moving around quite well now and swatting at the nurses with my walking stick if they don't bring my tea on time. They say I am making great progress, and they have me on a program of "physical jerks" to help my lungs. I should be doing the hurdles again shortly.

David, the orderly I told you about, who made the trip with me from the dressing station at the front to a proper hospital, dropped in again today. He's on his feet and will be shipped home any day. He's promised to stay in touch and to come to the country to see us. He and I have made a pact not to lose track of each other after what we have come through. I owe him a great deal.

Home soon, I hope.

Love,

Kernel

Dear Kernel:

Your father was down in the field below the house plowing with the team this afternoon when I saw him leave the horses and come hurrying up to the house waving his hat. I ran out to the veranda to see what was the matter. He shouted to me that the bells were ringing in Larkspur.

We both looked at each other and we just knew what it meant. Father ran to the barn and got Stormy and hitched him to the buggy, and we went hurtling down the hill to Larkspur like a pair of lunatics. Everyone was standing in the street and cheering and we learned that it was true. The war is over!

I have said a prayer each and every evening since you left us and now all my prayers are answered. God speed you home to us.

All our love,

Mother

By the time Kernel read this last letter, which had been "returned to sender," he was back home on Hall's Hill, having rejoined his chums for their Larkspur homecoming. Ms. Cameron showed me the clipping from the *Free Press & Economist*.

January 19, 1919

The Hog Special puffed its way down the Pine River Valley on Thursday morning to the Larkspur train station where a large and expectant crowd waited for its arrival. As soon as the whistle sounded in the distance, the Petunia Valley Foot Regimental Band burst into a spirited rendition of "The Prince Consort March" and played with great feeling until the train came to a halt and the returning soldiers spilled out onto the platform.

No eyes were dry as wives and husbands, mothers and sons, sisters and brothers found each other. Even the band members faltered one by one before this moving scene and found themselves unequal to the demands of keeping a wind instrument in operation.

"It must have been quite a moment," I said, putting the clipping down.

"There's an old story in our family," said Ms. Cameron. "They say that Jack Hall was searching around on the platform for his son and walked right past a tall man with white hair and a cane. The man reached out, caught Jack's arm, and said, 'Dad, it's me.' Jack stopped and looked at Kernel and his eyes filled with tears.

"And he said, 'Good God, boy! What have they done to you?'"

In the closing pages of the original edition of *With Axe and Flask*, my grandfather again narrows the focus of the story.

Kernel went back to the farm on Hall's Hill and married Sarah Cameron, one of Wim Cameron's sisters. [This would be Doreen's great-aunt, the one who gave her grandfather the letters.] They were happy enough

and raised two sons. His health did not allow him to
farm actively, but he pastured a herd of purebred Black
Angus cattle and served for many years as the township
clerk. During the 1920s, several distinguished visitors
made the journey to Hall's Hill, among them General
Arthur Currie, General Andrew McNaughton, and
even Viscount Byng of Vimy, who was then serving a
term as Canada's governor general. There is a picture
of Byng and Kernel Hall in the Larkspur Legion
Hall. They are standing under a shade tree beside an
enormous black bull on a lead shank. Scribbled in the
corner of the photo are the words: "To Kernel and
'Sir Douglas Haig,' with warm affection, Bungo."

A little further down, in terribly faded print that I had
previously skipped over, I found this:

On his very last day in France, Kernel Hall made the
acquaintance of a young medical orderly. They met in
a field dressing station in Flanders in January 1918
when Kernel presented himself with a nasty wound.
The roles of doctor and patient were quickly reversed
when a stray artillery shell obliterated the station.
The two men spent the next thirty-six hours on
stretchers beside each other as they were evacuated
by train and boat back across the Channel.

That orderly lived to attend medical school and
eventually came to Persephone as the general practi-
tioner in the village of Larkspur. In the years since
then, the doctor has had the pleasure of delivering
Mr. Hall's two sons and has shared many pleasant
afternoons fishing on the Pine River with his old
friend and his boys.

I turned and found Ms. Cameron leaning over my shoulder, reading the same passage.

"The orderly was my grandfather," I said. "It was because of Kernel Hall that he came to Persephone."

"How strange," she said. "And now your grandfather has done the same thing for you."

After reading this passage, I set the work aside for a bit and took a long walk down to the end of Wellington Street, where it crosses the Pine River. I sat on the bridge for a long time. I remember very well splashing in these waters as a ten-year-old boy with an excitable water spaniel while my grandfather stood in the shallows and pretended to fish.

My grandfather's history comes to a close on a wistful note. As he was writing the final paragraphs of his book in 1934, the Great Skid was in its seventh decade and there was no end in sight.

The discharged soldiers who descended from the train at Larkspur to embrace parents and loved ones changed Persephone just in the act of coming home. They were tough, observant, deeply skeptical of all authority, and devoted to one another. The bonds they had forged in the trenches were the strongest human attachments they would ever know.

They returned as usual to a land of limited opportunity. As soon as the war ended, the production of warships in the drydock ceased. The dead hand of Temperance had fallen on the land, closing the old Larkspur Distillery and forcing the last of the taverns on the New Military Road into new incarnations as boarding houses and storage sheds. The returning soldiers looked at one another and asked themselves, "What did we fight this war for, if not our freedoms?"

They set to work with a will and rebuilt the distillery in the privacy of the Pluto Marsh, and within a year, Persephone was once again shipping a large quantity of rye whisky to Montreal and south of the border. "Blind pigs" [illegal bars] sprang up in every driving shed in the county, despite the vigilance of the authorities.

Impatient with old rules and still capable of raising a ruckus on a Saturday night, they brought a new radicalism to politics and the workplace wherever they went. In 1919, they voted the provincial Tories out and sent a strange coalition of farmers and labour leaders to office. Still, the township could hardly contain their ambitions, and before long, the Hog Special resumed its one-way cargo of young people out of the township, many of them eager to try their fortunes in the west.

This steady exodus drained what little energy was left out of Persephone. Huge gullies now scarred the slopes of the Great Rift and sand blew in the air all summer. Farms accumulated debt, the farmers defaulted on their taxes, and the road system began to deteriorate. A spur line of the Hog Special railway running northwest into Pluto Township, used only to transport bootleg liquor, was ripped up and sold for scrap. Plans for rural electrification, talked about so optimistically before the war, were postponed indefinitely. By the end of the 1920s, the only export out of Persephone was the amber whisky made in the marshes.

Then the Depression hit.

The golf courses of Persephone are noted for their hazards, both natural and unnatural. Some golfers who tee off in the drumlins, with their deceptively manicured fairways, unexpected greens, cleverly camouflaged sand traps, and unexplored rough, have never been heard from again.

Chapter 9

THE COMING OF THE WEEKENDERS

1930 TO THE PRESENT

———•◆•———

Having come to the end of Dr. Goulding's history, I was still not quite sure why his painstaking work should receive such short shrift in his community. It's true, he exposed a few scoundrels and must have reminded everybody why certain families sit on opposite sides of the hall at church suppers. But was this enough to justify burying the last of his history books with him?

Doreen says she has actually found a few people who are now admitting to having read Dr. Goulding's book, and she says they found it discomfiting to be put under the spotlight. "It was a different time," she explains. "In those days, people just didn't think it was seemly to discuss in public where a person's family came from, how they made their money, or, worse, how they lost it. It made everybody squirm."

"But how do they feel now?"

"Probably the same," she said. She leaned over and pinched my arm.

"Ouch," I cried.

"You're going to need a thicker skin," she smiled, and she walked out with a stack of old newspapers.

That's the risk, isn't it? When you examine your own history properly, it does offer a rich source of speculation about why you have turned out so badly. Oh well, I'm not running for office.

Dr. Goulding rested his pen shortly after the Great Depression took hold in the world outside Persephone. So it falls to me to pick up the pen where he put it down.

Persephonites were better prepared than most Canadians for the Great Depression, having lived without folding money for the better part of sixty years. The futility of chasing after riches in a place like this stimulated people to use their imaginations and cultivate all sorts of delightful eccentricities.

In the dry summer of 1933, a farmer named Alvin Currie, who later became warden of the county, struck a large obstruction while grading a slough on the sixth concession at Highway 13. He and his brother Bob dug down into the clay and unearthed a rib bone four feet long, belonging to some prehistoric creature of great size. Before they could continue their digging, the rains came and the slough filled up again. That year, Alvin and Bob displayed the rib bone at the Larkspur Fall Fair, creating great excitement in the community. Two years later, during another dry summer, practically every able-bodied person in the township turned out to assist the brothers in a full-scale excavation of the swamp, which turned up another seventy bones. Alvin carted the skeletal remains away to his driving shed and worked for the next two months in great secrecy, refusing to allow even his brother into the workshop. Finally he unveiled his creation in a tent at the Larkspur Fall Fair, charging five cents a head for a glimpse of the "Monster of

Mildew Creek." This irritated a number of people who had participated in the digging, including Alvin's brother Bob, but nobody said anything. Some doubt about the authenticity of the bones was raised when a paying customer pointed out that one of the sabre teeth had a serial number and the words "Massey-Harris" stamped on the underside.

Alvin indignantly replied that this was where the teeth should go according to the book, and in the absence of the actual teeth he had constructed substitutes, using pieces off an old cultivator, a technique he claimed was entirely in keeping with accepted museum practices. The crowd demanded their money back, and Alvin and Bob got into a fistfight. The man who had identified the false tooth introduced himself as a professor of vertebrate paleontology from the Royal Ontario Museum in Toronto and questioned Currie's claim that he had discovered a sabre-toothed tiger. He offered to examine the bones at his own expense and return them assembled to the Curries.

Alvin figured this was a good deal, so he packed up the bones and sent them off on the train to the museum in Toronto. The scientists needed about half an hour to conclude that the bones actually constituted the hindquarters of a woolly mammoth. It was a significant find, they said, and they would be very interested in putting the entire skeleton on display, when and if it turned up. Until then the museum would keep the partial remains in storage.

Alvin Currie spent the rest of his life waiting for the swamp to dry up again, but it never did. In his declining years he tried without success to find a home for the bones in the township. No one was interested in the back end of a mammoth. The partial skeleton mouldered in the basement of the ROM in Toronto until the very dry summer of 1980, when Alvin's grandson Orval Currie discovered a tusk while attempting to contain a nuclear waste incident on the property. The community turned out once again, this time to unearth the front end of the mammoth. Thanks to a grant from the provincial Employment Development Fund, the complete skeleton is now on display in the Seniors' Lounge of the Larkspur Curling Rink.

The Currie Mammoth is typical of the sort of distraction that helped Persephonites through the dark days of the 1930s. Even at the worst of the slump, Port Petunia and Larkspur managed to hang onto a small collection of businesses, most of them owned by descendants of Tom Lynch in Port Petunia and by the MacKelvey family in Larkspur. With a lot of time on their hands, people began to reflect on their lives and look critically at the landscape, which by then was in a pretty dreadful state of despoliation. There were a handful of Persephonites in 1930 who remembered the great pines and spruces of the wilderness forest and how they used to give shelter from the Westerlies. They'd heard the stories about camping under them at night and picking the wildflowers along the little streams that once trickled down the sides of the Rift to feed the Boyne, Pine, and Petunia Rivers. By the early 1930s, many of the abandoned highland farms overlooking the bay had reverted to the township for unpaid taxes. Now all they produced was clouds of sand that swept down from their fallow fields into the streets of Port Petunia and Larkspur.

It was also a time of heartbreak because of the complete collapse of agriculture – let us not forget that Clarence Haddock, a great-great-grandson of Fanny and Bertram, now in his eighties, recalls that the years of the Depression were so dry that "grasshoppers sat on the rail fences with tears in their eyes and never crossed a field without a canteen." Even if a crop did succeed, there was no guarantee of a market. One fall, Clarence took a wagonload of apples with a team and wagon into Port Petunia, where he was offered so little for the apples that he refused to sell them. He turned the wagon around, and when he reached the town limits he pulled the pin on the tailgate, letting the apples roll out onto the highway.

There is a photo in the Municipal Office in Hollyhock of a group of men in suits standing on a sand dune, planting a white pine seedling in the spring of 1933. Handling the spade is old Jack Hall, founding chairman of the Persephone Township Reforestation Committee. Beside him stands his son Kernel, now the township clerk, and a group of councillors. You can almost feel the wind that whips around their trouser legs and snatches at their fedora hats. The photograph's caption informs us that they are gathered on one of the abandoned farms in the highlands to inaugurate a new county forest. The provincial historical plaque that marks the spot today (on the side of the road at Concession 6, Lot 15) stands in the shade of white pines and spruce nearly fifty feet high. It will be several more generations before you will be able to camp under them during the summer with your family, but it's a good start. Over the years, the Pine River Conservation Authority, the Watershed Biological Trust, the Boy Scouts and Girl Guides, and recently the representatives of the World Biosphere Protection Agency have joined forces to plant out more than a million trees.

Many public service groups that cater to Persephone's residents owe their origins to these hard times. Kernel Hall and Stu Fisher founded the County Farmers' Co-op in 1931 in a direct challenge to the big feed companies who dictated the price of grain, feedstuffs, and farm supplies. They led the farmers along the Pine River in the push for better ways to market beef, pork, poultry, and dairy products in the province. Several of these farmers volunteered to serve on the early livestock and crop associations that were the forerunners of today's marketing boards. When the federal government finally set up the supply management system for dairy and poultry products in the 1960s, their names crop up again as founding directors. In the less progressive highlands, the Haddock sons married local girls and produced a generation of resilient and resourceful drumlin farmers that Bertram Haddock would have hardly recognized. In the 1960s, descendants of Bertram and Fanny were among the first to appear in court charged with defying the new supply management system, with hunting out of season, and with growing their own smoking material.

Likewise, many of the ritual events Persephonites now celebrate got their start during those Depression years. The men of St. Luke's Anglican Church held the first Wild Game Dinner in 1930 and haven't missed a year since then. In the 1950s, they went further afield in search of moose, taking the train to Northern Ontario, but they were eventually banned from the railway for immodest behaviour and had to refit an ancient schoolbus for the purpose.* The Persephone Township Moose Bus sits up on blocks for the rest of the year and doubles as a clubhouse for the Larkspur Gun Club.

Another long-standing tradition is the Brucellosis Dance. In January 1954, a young veterinarian from the Ministry of Agriculture named Cato McCloskey visited the

---

* They actually got a moose in 1967, the same year the Maple Leafs last won the Stanley Cup. But they hit it on the highway on the way home, and the Ontario Provincial Police, who had also been skunked on their hunt that year, appropriated it. Some say that the Leafs must win the cup again to break the moose hunt jinx.

Larkspur Orange Lodge to give a lecture on the eradication of brucellosis, a disease of cattle. After the lecture was over, the lodge members cleared away the chairs and held a dance and a late supper. They had so much fun that evening, they decided to invite the young man back the following year to repeat the event, this time with a lecture on warble fly control. By the late 1960s the event was so deeply engraved on the township social calendar that it easily survived the eradication of the disease for which it had been named. After a long and productive career, Dr. McCloskey retired recently to Larkspur. He continues to give his annual lecture at the Orange Lodge in mid-January, the most recent being a slide show on manure management for livestock producers. The dance follows.

As Gertrude Lynch, retired obstetrical nurse from the Larkspur hospital and a great-granddaughter of Tom Lynch, recalls, "We had everything in those days except money." The churches ran their fowl and strawberry suppers, the cow clubs had their picnics, and the neighbours always managed to get together at corn roasts and sleigh rides. Every sideroad supported a stitch club, a baseball team, a hockey rink, and a horseshoe pitch. Since no one owned anything, every enterprise of public benefit had to be accomplished with wide community assistance, drawing from what people had to offer and could afford. In most cases, this was limited to spare time and the produce of the fields. In time, the ladies of the parish learned to throw together a supper for two hundred in their sleep, turning over the tables in the lodge for three sittings. The MacNebb Family Orchestra installed itself as the headline band at the lodge. As the band members aged, people learned to dance slower. Volunteer work parties turned up at public buildings to repair loose eavestroughs and rotting shingles. At community events of every kind, men, women, and children learned to step into their accustomed roles like the most obedient dairy cows plodding to their stanchions at milking time.

This was the era that saw the formation of the plowing clubs to teach new tillage techniques to conserve the precious topsoil – at least what little remained. The Woman's Christian Temperance Union began holding joint meetings with the Women's Institute and the Horticultural Society, gradually shedding its morbid interest in abstinence for the more constructive business of improving domestic science.

The Depression ended in most places when the Nazis invaded Poland. But Persephone would have to wait quite a while longer. World War II came as no surprise to the old soldiers of the township. They knew the work of 1914 was unfinished, and they stoically sent their sons off to fight another war. At the end of this one, only nine boys failed to return, which might suggest either that it was a safer war or that Persephone didn't do its part. Neither was the case. The young men from Persephone made skilled aircraft mechanics, shipwrights, munitions workers, radio operators, and merchant seamen. The bulk of the casualties came, as usual, from the ranks of the infantry – most of them in yet another ill-conceived frontal assault on a fortified position, the harbour of Dieppe. The others fell in the march up the boot of Italy and in the deadly sweep across the Scheldt Estuary.

In February 1946, an East European refugee named Bernard Burgener stepped off the train in Port Petunia and hiked to the top of Pipesmoke Mountain. He then strapped two boards on his feet, put two poles in his hands, and slid all the way down the snow-covered hill to the milk house door of Dougald MacEachern's barn. Dougald's surprise was nothing compared with his astonishment at the offer that Burgener subsequently made him for the farm. That summer, Bernie cleared a path down the hill and constructed a rope tow powered by a winch set up at the top. In the fall of 1947, he opened the Halcyon Ski Club and charged twenty-five cents a trip up the mountain on the rope tow. This created some hilarity in the beverage room of the Grand Central Hotel in Port Petunia. Until then, the steep slope of the Rift just below the granite cliff face was regarded as an obstruction to development, not a source of it. If it came up in discussion at all, it was referred to as "the back of the farm," or "where the road ends" or "where we last saw the cows." Here was a man who seemed to think people had nothing better to do than slide down the hill like a bunch of otters.

Then one Friday night the Hog Special arrived with a load of young swells from the city. They were happy to give Bernie his twenty-five cents a trip, and they kept the Kingbird Café hopping all day Saturday and Sunday bringing coffee and sandwiches out to the hill. Persephone had a new industry.

The trickle of visitors soon turned into a flood. Three more ski operators opened new runs and clubhouses, selling memberships and building lots on the land at the base of the hill. At first, the residents grumbled about being wakened at all hours of the night to start a tractor and tow a car out of the ditch for a sozzled skier who had missed the turn on the Town Line. They referred to the skiers as "sliders" and "slope dopes" and shook their heads in disgust. Then the men found work at $2 an hour running the snow groomers and the chairlifts. Their wives took over the kitchens in the ski lodge restaurants. New tractors appeared in the fields, and the wood trim on some of the red brick farmhouses got a fresh coat of paint. The Great Skid was finally over. You could say that it came to a halt at the bottom of a ski hill.

Prosperity brought great changes to the township. Farmers suddenly found themselves circling the block looking for a parking space in front of the Grand Central Hotel. When the town decided to install parking meters, several farmers took the law into their own hands, led a tractor brigade into town, hooked chains onto the meters, and yanked every one of them out of the pavement. This caused a certain amount of commotion, and it was some time before the town returned to normal. But the farmers had made their point, and that is why there have never been any parking meters on the main streets of Port Petunia or Larkspur or anywhere else in the township. It also explains why you can never find a parking place during business hours.

Folly continues to animate Persephone's municipal, provincial, and federal representatives, who somehow believe that some modern equivalent of the railway or the Extractor will transform its economy into a new Silicon Valley. The efforts of the township's politicians have left a legacy of rusted-out hulks from several auto parts factories that operated tax-free until the grants ran out. The province helped to build the dinosaur theme park on Highway 13 in the 1970s, through a low-interest loan to a consortium of developers who later did a stretch at Millhaven for manipulating trust funds. The dinosaurs did not carry the correct snow load rating and great chunks have fallen off them, making it look as if the Tyrannosaurus rex has just passed through Colonel Fortescue's Extractor. Despite warnings from a marine architect, they are now about to refloat the

Mary Anne from her watery grave outside the breakwall of the harbour and turn her into a casino.*

The average citizens, if there are such people in Persephone, remain unmoved by these ecstatic visions. They rise early and do chores, open their shops, file into their accustomed places in the Red Hen Restaurant, or hustle children down to the school bus, much the same way they've been rising and getting on with their lives around here since the Woodland Era. Which reminds me of the area's World Biosphere Reserve designation, which celebrates the rich diversity of rare and endangered species that make a home in this township. Maybe this designation has a significance beyond the preservation of the pink ladyslipper orchid, the endangered Persephone pine, or the almost-extinct Rift rattlesnake. It just might be official confirmation that there is a place here for exotic examples of the human species as well. Like myself.

All of Persephone's people are immigrants to this place. Even those who were born here have to listen to its voices and discover it for themselves. My grandfather, the scientist, spent a good part of his life trying to capture its essence and describe it – first in his grand history book and later in daily swipes with a butterfly net as he made his rounds. I think he understood by the end of his life that Persephone could never be fully captured in print. It cannot be studied in school or preached from a pulpit or found in editorials of the *Free Press* or the *Gleaner*. The essence of the place must be patiently absorbed over a lifetime, with the same care that a person might take in gathering the fragile

---

* After many more close calls, she finally crashed and sank and became part of the breakwall in the late 1800s.

elderberries of the Upper Pine River Valley and combing them gently into a pie crust. It appears suddenly like a dragonfly on the farm pond, hovers for an instant, and is gone. You'll hear a snip of it in the Red Hen Restaurant after the hot beef sandwiches have been cleared away or in a whisper as you stand in line at the counter of Dry Cry MacKelvey's Feed and Seed. It will come to you as a line of poetry overheard as you contemplate a broken axle on a fully loaded manure spreader or an overturned load of hay. Or it may manifest itself in the moment of clarity just after you wake up face down on the driveway after a late night at the Larkspur Gun Club, remembering a line from the smoke-filled daze of the night before.

You can find clues to the real Persephone through the folk wisdom passed along by an oral tradition of pithy remarks, epigrammatic expression, and dry witticism directed at everyone and no one in particular. For me, it begins with observations like "It takes poor land to make a good farmer." Such sayings carry the distilled wisdom of seven generations of Persephone residents. Collectively, like the Torah, the Bible, and the Koran, they contain much wisdom on secular issues like debt management ("Pay the neighbours first and let the oil company go hang"), construction ("We're building a fence, not a piano"), hired help ("Never hire a man with untied shoes"), and car insurance ("You shouldn't drive anything you can't afford to walk away from"). And like those sacred texts, they remind us that we are at the mercy of a jealous and capricious God who is quick to smite and slow to bless.

This communal wisdom offers comfort in the face of adversity, consolation in the face of defeat, realism in the face of exasperated expectations. The worst sin a man can confess to is surprise that things didn't work out better. The greatest triumph is to be thought of as a good neighbour.

As I have learned by listening to its voices past and present, the best hope for Persephone's future will not be found in any synergistic federal-provincial-private-sector boondoggle, but in the people themselves. Today, all races, colours, and creeds inhabit the township, and they are its true strength. Persephonites are famous as a fractious and disputatious people. They are urban, they are rural, they are permanent and they are seasonal, they are professional and they are blue-collar, they are sportsmen and they are artists. The only thing they agree about is Toronto.

The descendants of the founding families are everywhere. The Fortescues inhabit various pieces of land and old houses, living in genteel poverty despite the ambitions of their ancestor, Charles Augustus, and his sons, Lionel and Reggie. The Fortescues think of themselves as the hereditary aristocrats of the community, but they are alone in this opinion. The MacKelveys still have a reputation for sharp dealing, thanks to the patient acquisitions of Big Sandy and his descendants, and they now own all the land on the Pine River through Larkspur plus various feed mills, building supply outlets, several factories in Port Petunia, and a good chunk of the main street in both towns. The civic-minded Halls can be found on the hospital board and the service clubs; they lend a helping hand to everyone. The Pargeters have evolved into the last big farm operation in the township. They farm pretty much everything now with a fleet of Deathstar combines and monster tractors. The Bells still own all the newspapers, but they make their living down in the city. The old Glen Islet families are still clannish and cautious of outsiders. They are careful and quiet and entertain themselves chiefly in perpetuating old feuds in the families, which by now cannot be distinguished from one another without a laptop link to the genealogical Website. Scratch a MacNabb and you'll find a MacNebb, as they say.

Five generations have made a dramatic change in the Haddock family. It is difficult to credit the idea that an ineffective gentleman pioneer produced the resourceful group who cling to the drumlins like the tough blue chicory flower and the devilweed that thrives along the roadsides of the highlands. Clarence Haddock's son Freddy, a great-great-great-grandson of Fanny and Bertram Haddock and one of the last "mixed" farmers on the Seventh Line, practises as many as seven different trades in the same day. He is also a poet who favours iambic pentameter. The view property partially cleared by his ancestors is now one of the most valuable parcels on the edge of the Great Rift and was recently purchased by a dot-com millionaire who built a ten-thousand-square-foot house where the Haddock log shanty originally stood.* The Haddock homestead itself has been moved down the hill to the Port Petunia fairgrounds and is maintained as a living museum of pioneer days. To a certain breed of modern writer, it remains a place of pilgrimage.

Recently the population of Persephone Township clicked over the high last reached in 1850. Although farming has declined in importance and occupies only a handful of families, the Agricultural Society is thriving in the hands of volunteers, many of whom have only have a distant connection to the land. The president is a pharmaceutical salesman, and even I have been invited to become a member. Life goes on.

In some ways, the township is easier to reach than ever. You can tap into an Internet weather site and see a satellite

---

* There is a "For Sale" sign on it and the electricians have not been paid.

radar image that clearly shows the Great Rift and the Petunia River. In other ways it is as remote as always. It is a strange sensation as you zip along the back roads out towards Pluto Lake on a winter night to push the "scan" button on the car radio and watch it go around and around the dial without picking up a single station.

Just before this book went to press, I accompanied Doreen Cameron to the Larkspur Fall Fair, which has been held on the Hall-Pargeter-Bell homestead site without interruption since 1855. The weather was lovely, still and clear – a perfect September day for the opening ceremonies, which always include the Founders' Parade with its ritual re-enactment of the Great Trek and the arrival of the pioneers in Larkspur. There is a mathematical theory of genetics that says we are all related to Queen Nefertiti of ancient Egypt. This principle would appear to apply to Persephone in spades. So many of us are now related to those first families that they have to recruit volunteers to sit in the grandstands and serve as spectators to the parade. Doreen and I were happy to oblige.

It was a great fair. Alligator wrestling is the latest nifty addition to the program of special events, and the self-propelled combine demolition derby drew a big crowd. I was amazed by the diversity and novelty on the grounds. I asked Doreen how the Ag Society gets liability insurance coverage for events like the Mutton-Busting Sheep Rodeo for the kids, the Junior Farmers Jousting Jersey Tournament, midget wrestling, the Piano Toss, and the last horse race at a fall fair in Ontario. She said, "We don't."

There is a tacit understanding among the members that if anyone ever mentions the word "liability," the meeting is adjourned. The society owns no property apart from the ghastly site where the fair is held, has never put up a proper building, and never declares a profit. If any money is left over after the President's Reception on the Tuesday following the fair, the secretary has instructions to donate it to the Terpsichore Society, whose presidency is currently held by Adelaide Smart's great-great-granddaughter Courtney. Doreen says, "If we get sued, our only asset is a piece of reclaimed swamp, and they can have it."

This is why you still see old-fashioned life-threatening delights such as horse races and the llama steeplechase at the Larkspur Fall Fair. For three days each September, the air is filled with the sound of children's laughter and the steady drone of Ernie Hall's voice over the PA system, marshalling the events and announcing highlights of the day. The parade arrives in front of the grandstand and the township flag flutters to the top of the pole. Then the Petunia Valley Foot Regimental Band plays "See the Conquering Hero Comes" and "O Canada." Doreen says she still gets a lump in her throat when she hears Ernie break into the middle of the anthem with the command: "The horses are coming around . . . *Mothers*, get your children *off* the *track*!"

As we wandered among the crowds, Doreen spotted an ancient lady sitting by the grandstand in a wheelchair. It was Rita MacKelvey from the nursing home. We stopped for a chat. Miss MacKelvey asked how my book was coming and if I'd got the story of the curse down right. I told her I'd done my level best. While she and I were visiting, it occurred to me that this woman actually knew people who had crossed the ocean in tall ships and cleared trees from some of Persephone's drumlin farms. She is a living link between the time of the pioneers and us. I wondered if she saw any sign that the community might finally be coming to understand that it has to stop looking at

Persephone as a place to be mined out and sold off to the highest bidder. I bent over and looked intently into her furrowed face and realized that I would find no answers there. The answers, if there are any, lie in the present.

The way I see it, now that I've retraced by grandfather's footsteps and taken a few tentative steps of my own, is that the Michael Bliss historical paradigm is still very much at work in Persephone. The opportunities may not be quite so limited, but more than a 2 to 3 percent return on any investment is something only a weekender would understand. Human experience is not transferable. Each generation must start from scratch and learn the same painful lessons. But it would be nice to think that the next generation will come to see Persephone as a place their children and grandchildren might not need to escape from. I wonder what my grandfather would say about that.

The new Persephone is building on the foundations of the old, and it looks like that may include me. When I bumped into the mayor of the amalgamated Township of Hillview at the duck race, he suggested that I would make life a lot easier for everybody all around if I would just ask the council to sign my grandfather's property back to the family. I pictured the sagging yet pretty house, and for the first time since I came back here, it looked more like an opportunity than a headache. I told him I would give it some serious thought.

Doreen and I are off this afternoon to watch the Larkspur Lacrosse League play the Demeter Shamrocks on one of the old tavern sites on the New Military Road (which has been four-laned as a bypass around Port Petunia to accommodate the winter ski traffic). Tonight we'll have dinner at the Laughing Waters Steak House and Pasta Bar in Hollyhock – they have yet another new chef and we're curious to check him out; then we'll drop by the dance in the Fortescue Beach Palladium. After that? Well, we'll probably take a drive out to the very end of Port Petunia Drydock Park and watch the waves lap gently over the wreck of the *Mary Anne*. Unless the wind gets up, of course . . .

This text of this book is set in Cochin and its display type is Birch. Cochin originated with the Peignot Foundry in Paris about 1915. It is based on the lettering of eighteenth-century French copperplate engravers and was adapted by Monotype in 1917, followed by ATF in 1925. The roman is distinctive but the italic is even more so, being closer to formal handwriting or engraving than most italics.

Illustrations: p. 6: the author; p. 22: *Portrait of Archibald McNab* (oil, anonymous) is reproduced with permission of the Royal Ontario Museum © ROM; p. 54: Robin Sheard Nyikos; p. 78: Gord Handley, photographer; p. 108: Province of Ontario Archives, Toronto; p. 140: John Knox, photographer (with thanks to Bill Copeland as Fortescue); pp. 172 and 202: courtesy of the Dufferin County Museum; p. 232: John Knox, photographer (with thanks to Tony Hendrie, Douglas Rowland, and "Lily" Pankhurst).

Map by Shelagh Armstrong-Hodgson

Book design by Blaine Herrmann